ROSES

To Rosie: who, until fairly recently, didn't like roses.

ROSES

Michael Marriott

CONTENTS

6

Introduction

16

Rose inspiration

60

Rose types

86

Rose selector

204

Rose care

introduction

The romance of the rose

For thousands of years, roses have been valued for their beauty, perfume, and for their use in medicine. They often symbolize love, both human and spiritual.

Images of five-petalled flowers that could be roses can be seen on pottery shards found in the Jiangsu region of China dating back to 5000 BCE. They feature in Egyptian wall paintings and hieroglyphs from 2500 BCE, as well as in Ancient Greek and Roman writings. The Greek scientist and philosopher Theophrastus, born around 371 BCE, wrote about the wild dog rose, as well as varieties with twelve, twenty, or even a hundred petals. This gives us an early insight into roses' habit of readily mutating and crossing with one other to produce new variants – a natural consequence that occured once roses were transplanted from the wild into gardens.

Roses in Asia

Confucius (551–479 BCE) tells of roses being grown in the Imperial gardens in Beijing. Later, during the Han dynasty (206 BCE–220 CE), wild roses were grown on the palace walls. By the Tang dynasty (618–906 CE), the Chinese were known to be expert rose growers, and during the next dynasty, the Song, serious rose breeding began, before reaching its height during the Ming dynasty (1368–1644). The *Qun Fang Pu* (*Cyclopaedia of Flowers*) by Wang Xiangjin, published in 1621, mentions many of the 100 or so roses that were grown in China at that time.

While the category of "China rose" is well established (p.72), the names of individual Chinese varieties were actively disregarded by western horticulturists when they brought these roses back to European markets. Thus, Mu Hsiang (Grove of Fragrance) became *Rosa banksiae*, while Yue Ji (Four Season Rose) was dubbed *Rosa chinensis*.

The Persian Prince Humay Meeting the Chinese Princess Humayun in a Garden
As its name suggests, this gouache artwork, painted in c.1450 and part of the Islamic School, depicts love at first sight in a rose garden.

In India during the 16th century, Emperor Shah Jahan was symbolized by a red rose, and there are many rose motifs on the walls of the Taj Mahal. The rose became known as a symbol for beauty: the Hindu god Vishnu is said to have created his bride, Lakshmi, from 108 large and 1,008 small rose petals. In southern India, the rose was central to the culture of both nobles and ordinary citizens of the Vijayanagara Empire (1336–1646). Abdur Razzak, a Persian diplomat, visited in 1443 and wrote, "Roses are sold everywhere. These people could not live without roses, and they look upon them as quite as necessary as food."

On the island of Java in Indonesia, roses looking very much like 'Cramoisi Supérieur' and an unknown blush rose are grown on a large scale for the Muslim festival of Eid, in which people adorn the graves of their relatives with the blooms. The flowers are also used for other ceremonies and celebrations, such as weddings.

Roses in Bud and Bloom with Butterflies and Insects This artwork, part of the Chinese School, is thought to have been painted in the 18th century.

Roses in Europe

The Greeks and Romans used roses in their cooking and cosmetics, which means they must have grown them on a fairly large scale. But roses also played an important part in their ornamental gardens: Pliny the Younger, describing a garden in a letter, wrote, "a visitor on entering would look over the rose garden, whose scent would reach him." They used roses enthusiastically for their various festivals, celebrations, and banquets. The rose was associated with Venus (and hence with sex), as well as excess. At Cleopatra's first meeting with Mark Antony, a layer of roses a cubit (half a metre/yard) deep covered the floor and others hung from the ceiling in festoons. There is also the perhaps apocryphal story that at a banquet given by the third-century Roman emperor Heliogabalus, so many roses were dropped from the ceiling that some people drowned.

Over time, the rose transformed from a pagan symbol, with unsavoury and decadent connotations in Roman and Greek life, to one that was central to both Christianity and Islam. It became a symbol for the Virgin Mary, who was described by the fifth-century poet Sedulius as the "rose among thorns". Perhaps the most obvious sign of the importance of the rose in Christianity are the magnificent rose windows in many churches and cathedrals. These are often dedicated to Mary and she is depicted sitting in the middle. At Westminster Abbey an inscription on the floor says (in Latin), "As the Rose is the flower of flowers, so is this the house of houses."

The allegorical *Roman de la Rose*, the story of a lover searching for his lady's love (the rose of the title), shows that in the 13th century the rose still stood for human (as well as spiritual) love. It describes a dream in which a lover is on a quest to pluck a rose, which he has seen on a rose bush reflected in the Fountain of Love at the centre of a walled garden. The poem became one of the most influential and controversial works of the Middle Ages.

On a more practical level, a late 13th-century storekeeper's records, found in the debris of a perfume workshop in the Frankish castle at Pylos in the south-western Peloponnese, show the trade in perfumed oils, including rose. This would have required the production of large numbers of blooms, and sophisticated equipment to produce the oil, and indicates how much rose perfume was valued.

The magic of scent

Most people's immediate reaction to seeing a rose is to smell it. Even young children are drawn to smelling roses. A deliciously fragrant rose has the wonderful ability to both calm us down and raise our spirits.

Fragrances are generally strongest after a period of warm weather and immediately following some light rain, when the atmosphere is humid. They often develop and change as a flower opens, so it's important not to judge a variety's fragrance by a single bloom: if the flower is too young or too old, it is unlikely to smell of anything. Smell each variety on a regular basis: fragrances will often change dramatically from hour to hour, day to day, season to season, and even year to year.

The strongest fragrance is likely to be found when the bloom is at its most beautiful, but it's worth smelling two or three flowers at slightly different stages to find the best and to discover the differences between them. Don't rush in and give the flower a quick, embarrassed sniff. Smell it and smell it again, trying to gather as much fragrance from it as possible. It doesn't matter if you can't identify the scent: simply enjoy it for what it is.

Fragrance is a crucial part of why roses became so popular, perhaps due to the wonderfully strong and delicious perfume found in *Rosa gallica* and the other old roses. There are five main groups of fragrances, each originating from different rose types. Apart from tropical epiphytic orchids, no other plant has such a wide range of completely different fragrance types.

Old rose fragrance

This is the archetypal rose fragrance. There are subtle differences to be found between the different groups of old roses (pp.68–71): the gallicas have a richer, heavier scent, whereas albas are lighter and sweeter. When found in more modern roses that have China roses in their parentage, like the Bourbons (p.73) and the English roses (p.82), a fruity element starts to appear.

Myrrh fragrance

The name is derived not from the biblical myrrh, but from the herb sweet cicely, *Myrrhis odorata*, which smells strongly of aniseed. This fragrance was found originally in the old rambler 'Splendens', descended from the white field rose, *Rosa arvensis*. From 'Splendens' came the pale pink gallica 'Belle Isis', which was one of the original parents that the British breeder David Austin used in his breeding programme, specifically as a parent to his first variety, 'Constance Spry', which has a strong myrrh scent. It has since found its way into many other English roses. Some people dislike it, and it is true that in some varieties it is almost too strong, but it can be delicious, especially when it is combined with other fragrances.

Roses
This artwork is by Albert-Tibule Furcy de Lavault (1847–1915), who is known for his still-life paintings of cut garden flowers.

> "Fragrance may be said to be the
> other half of the beauty of a rose."
> David Austin, *The English Roses*

Tea fragrance

Like the fresh tea leaves it's named after, this scent comes from China and the Far East, originally from breeding the vigorous climbing species *Rosa gigantea* with the bushy, repeat-flowering *R. chinensis*. It is found in more modern varieties, especially in some hybrid musks and English roses, but varies greatly, from a fresh violet fragrance to a harder, almost tarry one. A superb fragrance at its best.

Fruity fragrances

This covers a huge range of fruits, from apple, strawberry, raspberry, and damson through all the different citruses to tropical fruits like mango, guava, and lychee. These fragrances mostly come from two parents, *Rosa chinensis* and *R. wichurana*, and are often combined with other scents, especially old rose, to produce some truly delicious, almost mouth-watering perfumes. Many of the English roses have fruity fragrances.

Musk fragrance

While all the fragrances described above come from petals, musk comes from stamens and has the wonderful ability to waft on the air. It's particularly common in ramblers, which also have great numbers of small single or semi-double flowers and a large bunch of stamens in the middle. It is reminiscent of the musk fragrance widely used in perfumes. At close quarters it often smells of cloves. Some varieties have just the right combination of petals and stamens so that the musk can be appreciated alongside the fragrance of the petals.

Leaves and "moss"

It is not just rose flowers that have attractive fragrances. The young leaves of sweet briar, *Rosa rubiginosa*, have a delicious apple scent that is especially noticeable on warm summer evenings. It can be kept clipped to encourage as many young leaves as possible. The mossy growth around the buds of moss roses and the glandular hairs around the buds of gallicas are quite sticky and have an attractive, resinous smell.

The Soul of the Rose
This 1908 painting (also known as *My Sweet Rose*) by John William Waterhouse is thought to have been inspired by Alfred, Lord Tennyson's 1855 poem *Maud*.

ROSE
inspiration

Rose gardens

A rose bed or garden offers the most intense rose experience. Roses can be used to carpet the ground, provide a backdrop, and arch over the paths.

The first recorded plan for a "rosarium" was drawn up in 1813 by landscape gardener Humphry Repton for Ashridge House in Hertfordshire. It shows a number of coffin-shaped beds around a central fountain, set within a ring of rose-covered arches. At that time, though, there were few suitable roses for such a garden – proof, perhaps, that Repton didn't know his roses.

The development of hybrid tea roses in the mid-19th century sparked the fashion for formal rose gardens. Like the floribundas that followed, these new roses had a long flowering season, so the gardens were colourful throughout the summer months and into autumn. The French were some of their greatest proponents, with the magnificent Roseraie de l'Haÿ and the rose garden in the Parc Bagatelle botanic garden in Paris, begun in the 1890s and in 1905 respectively.

This new fashion became so dominant that until the late 20th century, roses were mainly planted in formal rose gardens or rose beds. In private gardens this could mean just a small circular bed, perhaps with a standard rose in the middle, or several beds set out in a symmetrical pattern. Every public park had a rose garden. Fungicides and pesticides were freely used to combat the pests and diseases that flourished in these monocultures. Later, as fashions changed (and gardeners learned to steer clear of toxic chemicals), the trend for mixed planting emerged (pp.24–33).

Planning a rose garden

While mixed plantings are beautiful, a well planted and maintained rose garden can still be superb. The beds need to be filled with roses, so that little or no soil is visible. This usually means planting them about 50cm (18in) apart, although larger varieties need more space, as do roses grown in warm climates. Individual beds can either be filled with one variety or, if space allows, a number of different ones. As far as colours go, the choices are wide, from pastel harmonies ('Queen of Sweden', 'Olivia Rose Austin', and 'Desdemona') to exuberant clashing kaleidoscopes ('Empereur Charles IV', 'Golden Beauty', and 'Lovely Parfuma').

Choose upright varieties so you can get between them in order to weed, dead-head, and so on. As this is a monoculture, they also need a high level of disease resistance. Repeat-flowering and fragrance are usually prerequisites too. This generally limits the choice to hybrid teas, floribundas, some English roses, and some Portlands.

A formal rose garden can be made to fit almost any space, the individual beds holding anything from just a few roses up to several hundred – as in Queen Mary's Gardens in Regent's Park, London, or Victoria State Rose Garden in Australia. It could be as simple as four beds surrounding a central

Roses in abundance
At the garden at David Austin Roses, Shropshire, this tapestry of modern shrub roses is backed by paler climbing varieties, and offset here and there by dark topiary pillars.

Modern formality
Every shade of pink rose, from
the palest bloom to a dark purple,
surrounds a formal fountain and
statue in a new rose garden at
Glyndebourne, Sussex.

"Obelisks and pillars can add height to a border. They also provide winter interest, when the roses grown up them are bare of flowers and leaves."

Two tiers together
Tall standards of 'Ballerina' are grown above the same rose in its natural shrub form, fronted by lavender and a clipped low hedge.

circular bed or water feature, edged with a low hedge – perhaps yew, lavender, or *Euonymus* 'Jean Hugues'. Box is traditional, but is risky nowadays due to box blight and box tree caterpillar, and its roots can seriously compete with those of the roses.

Adding height

Standard, or "tree", roses add an extra layer, either in the middle of the border or lining paths through the garden. They're sold with different stem lengths, to suit different positions. A full standard, with the flowers at about 1.2–1.5m (4–5ft), works well in most borders. Shorter stems can be useful for raised beds or containers, while weeping standards can make magnificent heaps of flowers. The stem itself is not very beautiful, so should be hidden by the other roses or plants around it. Standard roses need stout stakes to support their large heads. Sweet chestnut is particularly good for this purpose as it will last 40 years in the soil with no preservative.

Varying the planting

Rather than sticking to similar-sized roses, for a more informal look you could combine rose types of very different heights and growth habits. How about planting the hummock-forming 'Flower Carpet White' next to the taller, more upright 'Champagne Moment', or the rounded 'Scarborough Fair' with the taller, shrubbier 'Princess Alexandra of Kent'? You might include some roses for their hips or colourful leaves (pp.160–65), though avoid any species roses that tend to spread by suckering, such as hybrids of *R. spinosissima*, as they may take over your border. You could also back your border with rose-covered walls, or add a pergola over the path through it.

As a halfway house to the mixed border, space your roses more widely and interplant them with low-growing perennials or bulbs. Some believe that aromatic plants such as alliums, lavender, or salvias keep roses healthier; and of course spring bulbs will brighten the bed before the roses start to flower. Do keep the area under each rose free of competition, though.

Mixing it up

Planting roses with perennials, biennials, annuals, bulbs, and other shrubs opens up endless possibilities for contrasting shapes and colours, and creating atmospheric gardens.

Mixing roses with other plants may seem like a fairly new gardening practice, but in fact there was great enthusiasm for it in the late 19th and early 20th century. In his bestselling 1883 book *The English Flower Garden*, William Robinson railed against planting roses in rose gardens. He loved roses, writing that "the nobler flowers have been rejected as unfit for the flower garden [meaning the mixed border] in our day, and first among them the Rose." He goes on to say, "I begin the summer garden with the Rose, too long left out of her right place, and put in the background."

The mixed border has many advantages. It extends the flowering season, helps to keep the roses healthier, is a way of introducing blue into the colour scheme and, perhaps most importantly, enhances the beauty of the roses by juxtaposing them with contrasting plants. Most shrub roses have an informal habit, matching that of most perennials, biennials, and annuals. The only roses that can be tricky to include in a mixed border are the more formal hybrid teas, floribundas, patio, and miniature roses, all of which are generally better suited to other places in the garden.

A 50:50 mix of roses and perennials works well, but there's no reason why you can't add just one rose, especially one full of character like the beautiful rich pink damask 'Ispahan' or the free-flowering apricot 'Lady of Shalott'. For more impact, if you have the space, plant three specimens close together (about two-thirds their width apart) to give the impression of one big bush.

Planning a mixed border

If you're making a new mixed bed, or taking over a neglected garden that you've cleared in order to start over, you can design your planting around roses. Use them to structure the site: as a backdrop on walls and fences, to provide focal points, and to grow beside paths or even over arches. Once you've worked out where your structural roses should go, add complementary perennials and bulbs around them – perhaps with annuals as gap-fillers in the first year.

The first thing to consider when planning to mix roses with other plants is how much space they need. With the exception of the tough species roses

A mixed medley
Roses bloom throughout this colourful garden: shrub varieties bloom alongside euphorbia and delphiniums, a rambler grows through a tree, and the rear fence is clothed with climbing roses.

and their hybrids, roses don't like having other plants growing right round their base. Ideally, they should be planted far enough away that their outer edges just touch those of the rose, so that their flowers end up side-by-side. As a rough guide, add the suggested spreads for the rose and its proposed neighbour and then halve this total to work out the best planting spot. So the planting hole for a 1.2m (4ft) wide rose needs to be about 90cm (3ft) away from that for a 60cm (2ft) wide perennial. They won't be mature, or probably in flower, when you plant them, and this distance can easily seem too great – but it is necessary, since perennials and biennials often have extensive root systems that will take the lion's share of water and nutrients from the ground, leaving little for the rose.

Annuals can be planted closer. They have a smaller root system that won't interfere with that of the rose. They often have a very long flowering season, and can look lovely growing through roses. Try cosmos (pink, white, magenta, and even shades of yellow and orange), blue, white or pink love-in-a-mist (*Nigella*), and orange to ivory marigolds (*Calendula*), which are quite short, and so good in front of roses. One of the very best is *Phacelia tanacetifolia*, normally grown as a ground-cover plant. It grows

25

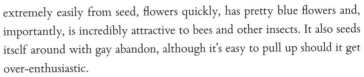

extremely easily from seed, flowers quickly, has pretty blue flowers and, importantly, is incredibly attractive to bees and other insects. It also seeds itself around with gay abandon, although it's easy to pull up should it get over-enthusiastic.

Many perennials have the nasty habit of flopping over and resting on their neighbours, something young rose bushes do not appreciate. *Nepeta* (catmint) 'Six Hills Giant' is a classic example: it grows too tall and then collapses in strong wind or heavy rain, smothering its neighbours. To be safe, choose a shorter variety like *N.* x *faassenii* 'Kit Cat'. Once roses are well established, a bit of gentle falling over (be it the rose or the perennial that leans) can look very pretty. Many of the gallicas have a fairly lax habit and can look beautiful with their flowers resting on their neighbours.

If you want to add some roses to an existing perennial border, beware of the illusionary gap. All too often, you'll identify an apparent space in a herbaceous border in winter or early spring, especially after pruning, and duly plant a rose in it. Perennials, though, are adept at filling spaces, and before too long the poor young rose will disappear under a tangle of stems. Make sure it is a real space in the border, and stake the perennials to stop them from flopping over, at least for the first year or two, until the rose can hold its own.

Combining plants

Roses are quite exceptional in having such a long flowering period. Most flower from late spring or early summer through to late autumn or early winter. To extend this season even more, spring bulbs are an obvious addition. Many flower from late winter into spring, when roses are at their barest, having just been pruned. (You'll need to take care to leave room to get to your roses to prune them without trampling your spring bulbs, though.)

It is, though, when roses and their neighbours flower at the same time that magical combinations are created. It is easy to plant a range of roses and other plants and hope for the best, but the art of creating truly beautiful borders lies in identifying good partners that set each other off. This is the fun part of gardening: difficult to achieve, but so rewarding when it works. You'll need to think about not just the colour, height, and shape of the plants, but their character. How close a plant is to the original wild species will determine how formal or informal it appears. A big wild rose will not go well with a highly bred *Echinacea* or *Antirrhinum*.

A living painting
In Yokohama English Garden, Japan, orange roses and rose hips mingle with the paler apricot shades behind, while the tall ornamental grasses, scarlet salvia, and silver-leafed tree provide depth and movement.

Try echoing the shapes of your roses: for example, you could interplant more upright roses, such as 'Queen of Sweden', 'The Lady Gardener', and 'James L. Austin', with foxgloves, delphiniums, and lupins – or contrast them with rounded plants like catmint, hardy geraniums, and herbaceous peonies. These might also hide the roses' bare legs, should they have them. Most shrub roses, though, have a more rounded, informal shape, so will contrast with tall, thin perennials or summer-flowering bulbs. Short, ground-hugging plants like Mexican fleabane (*Erigeron karvinskianus*), some hardy geraniums, and pinks (*Dianthus*) make perfect edging plants that fill the gap between the rose and the edge of the border.

Catching the sunlight
The bright pink blooms of 'John Clare' are here underplanted with lamb's ear and accompanied by Russian sage (right).

"When roses and their neighbours flower at the same time, magical combinations are created."

Consider flower size, too. Most roses have larger flowers than perennials, and you can choose plants that exaggerate this difference. For example, the large pink blooms of 'Olivia Rose Austin' look good next to catmint's small blue flowers. Later in the season, the myriad small flowers of *Symphyotrichum* (formerly *Aster*) 'Little Carlow' contrast beautifully with the wide, warm pink, open flowers of 'Eustacia Vye'. The reverse is possible, too: the small-flowered purple-pink rose 'Sibelius' with blowsy pale pink peony 'Sarah Bernhardt', or white 'Matchball' backed by hollyhocks.

The next consideration is height. To create the best colour combination, the blooms of the plants you're combining should end up close to each other, and in general taller plants work best behind shorter ones, especially if the border is being viewed just from one side; for example, if it's backed by a wall, fence, or hedge. But this shouldn't be made an absolute rule: it would be dull indeed if everything was in serried ranks, in strict height order from front to back. Height variation within the border will liven it up, and any rose with a good fragrance should be easily accessible for regular sniffing. Sometimes it is effective to look through a light, airy plant like the grass *Stipa gigantea* or the ornamental thistle *Cirsium rivulare* 'Atropurpureum' to the rose behind it.

The rather stiff, upright growth and brightly coloured, stylized flowers of most hybrid teas mean that they tend to clash with the traditional companions for roses, which mostly have small, softly coloured flowers and a relaxed growth habit. While perhaps not to everyone's taste, a mixture of brightly coloured hybrid teas, floribundas (such as 'Golden Beauty', 'Fruity Parfuma', and 'Natasha Richardson') and similarly vivid, upright companions could be fun – perhaps in a tropical-style garden.

There are some more informal, graceful hybrid teas with scented single flowers, such as apricot 'Mrs Oakley Fisher' and pink 'Dainty Bess', and others with flowers very much in the style of old roses, such as creamy yellow 'Concorde' and soft pink 'Amorosa'. All of these are much easier to weave into a mixed border. The floribundas offer more exceptions: white or pastel varieties like 'Iceberg' and 'Champagne Moment' associate easily with other plants, while 'Lovely Parfuma' and 'Caroline's Heart' both have pink flowers and would fit in well.

A rich combination The changing colours of *Rosa* x *odorata* 'Mutabilis' work well with the rather mysterious dark heads of *Allium sphaerocephalon*.

Colour effects

While it is of course possible to plant with no thought of colour association and end up in a glorious jumble, it's worth editing your palette down to find the best colour companions. You could combine shades that are close to each other, such as yellow and apricot, or opposites like yellow and purple. Fewer colours work especially well in small spaces.

Use intense colours if you want to create a powerful and exciting effect (though if you get the shades wrong, your mistake will be obvious): magenta 'Empereur Charles IV' with the late-flowering *Aster* x *frikartii* 'Mönch', or purple 'Sibelius' with a dark lupin such as 'Masterpiece'. Soft shades are much easier to combine: even if they are not ideal companions, the clash will not be so glaring. Try white 'Summer Memories' with one of the pale geraniums like mauve *G. renardii* or white *G. macrorrhizum* 'White-Ness', 'Eustacia Vye' with the pale pink *Astrantia* 'Buckland', or soft apricot 'Stéphanie d'Ursel' with the yellow, fragrant daylily *Hemerocallis* 'Lemon Bells'. If you feel a border of nothing but soft shades might look rather dull, use a stronger colour to add some lively focal points.

Soft contrasts
The blue hardy geranium sets off the soft pale colours of 'Emily Brontë' and white foxglove in this mixed bed.

"It's worth editing your palette
down to find the best colour
companions: neighbouring shades
like pinks and purples work well."

While it's all very well talking about how to create the perfect colour association, in practice it is difficult to do so accurately from pictures and descriptions. If you can, cut a flower from the rose you're trying to place and walk round your garden, or your local nursery, offering it up to other plants. This will give you a much better insight into the best combinations. Some will not work at all, others will look all right, and some will really spark off each other.

It's important to take account of all the different stages of a rose flower. The bud is often a quite different colour to the open flower, which may change dramatically again as it fades. Stand back to get an overall impression of the plant – you could seriously upset your carefully planned colour scheme if you get distracted by the stage (often the bud or new flower) that attracts you most.

Reinventing the shrubbery

A shrubbery has a rather old-fashioned, Victorian ring to it, conjuring up an image of an overgrown, gloomy, neglected corner. Instead, why not choose tall roses and other flowering shrubs to create a colourful, fragrance-filled spot with year-round interest. Some long-flowering, mostly tall, roses that would work here are soft yellow to pink *R. x odorata* 'Mutabilis', 'Clair Matin', deep pink 'Vanity', and pink and white 'Ballerina'; 'The Lark Ascending', 'Buttercup', 'Tottering-by-Gently', 'Morning Mist', and 'Penelope' also have hips.

Witch hazel (*Hamamelis*) would add winter flowers, acers and berberis good autumn leaf colour, spindle, berberis and skimmia winter berries. Buddleia, hydrangea, philadelphus, skimmia, and lavender would give extra flowers to complement the roses.

Precious jewels
Here, 'Gertrude Jekyll' is set off by sapphire delphiniums and *Salvia nemorosa* 'Amethyst' to create a rich assortment of complementary jewel tones.

Rose hedges

Whether planted with a single variety or several, a rose hedge can be magnificent. Or, inspired by wild hedgerows, you can make a mixed hedge of roses and other shrubs.

Roses can make a colourful, impenetrable boundary, or a low, fragrant internal divider. Substantial, wilder, thorny varieties, ones that don't necessarily repeat-flower but will set hips in the autumn, are a good choice for external boundaries. The classic is *Rosa rugosa* and its hybrids (p.161); they are particularly tough and healthy, flower over a long period, and many produce cherry tomato-sized hips. Other species roses and their near hybrids, or some of the more modern, small-flowered hybrid musk-like roses (such as 'Sweet Siluetta' and 'Grand-Duc Jean', with carmine-red flowers and a white eye) would also be excellent.

For an internal barrier, the best choice is a more upright, compact, and less thorny rose, ideally one with a good fragrance. Many English roses and floribundas, such as 'Queen of Sweden', 'The Lady Gardener', and 'Île de Fleurs' work well.

Blooming boundary
This hedge of the shrub rose 'Sea Foam' forms part of a large-scale landscaping project across the town of Aurora, New York, USA.

Bold choices
The vivid orange shades of 'Lady of Shalott' make for an eye-catching hedge at the gardens of David Austin Roses, Shropshire.

Since you are planting a row of roses – often of the same variety – quite closely together, it's important to choose ones with excellent disease resistance. As for spacing, an easy rule of thumb is to plant them half their width apart, so roughly 50cm (1½ft) apart for a rose that grows 1m (3ft) wide. They could go closer if you want to make a dense hedge quickly, or further apart if you're aiming for an airy, see-though screen.

For an informal look, combine roses of different heights and widths, or mix them with other shrubs, as happens naturally with wild roses. You could stick to species roses, mixed with honeysuckle, field maple, blackthorn and hawthorn, or use longer-flowering garden varieties that have a wild feel to them, such as 'Île de Fleurs' or 'Goldspatz', alongside *Lonicera periclymenum* 'Scentsation', *Lonicera × purpusii* 'Winter Beauty', and a small crabapple – 'Evereste', for example, can be pruned as a hedge.

Growing up & over

Roses are surely the best of all climbing plants. They are wonderfully variable and versatile, many are long-flowering and scented, and there is one to fit just about any vertical surface in the garden.

It is important to choose the right-sized variety for the position you want to grow it in. An over-vigorous rose will become a menace if grown up a small support. A correctly-sized variety may take longer to mature, but it will then be easy to maintain, flower more freely, and generally look right.

Covering walls & fences

Of all the places it is possible to grow roses, training them up the wall of a house, especially either side of the front door, must be one of the most common. Climbers are usually the best choice, as all but the shortest ramblers can be too vigorous and hard to manage on walls. Choose a variety with as long a flowering period as possible, or else extend the season of interest of a once-flowering rose by growing another climber, such as a clematis, through it.

The colour of the rose's flower needs to work with the colour of the wall. A warm pink or white usually goes with red brick, but it's safest to hold a flower up against the wall to see if it works. Painted walls and fences are easier, but it is still important to consider colour: a pale rose on a pale background won't create much of an impact. Instead, how about a deep pink or purple rose – 'Gertrude Jekyll' or 'Purple Skyliner' – for a white or cream wall, or yellow or apricot – 'Golden Gate', 'Ghislaine de Féligonde', or 'Lady of Shalott' – against a soft yellow wall. And don't forget that unpainted fences are liable to fade to grey as they age.

For a 2m (6ft) fence, look at climbers up to 3m (10ft) tall (they'll be fanned out against the fence) or the larger shrub varieties, which will easily grow to that height, especially against a warm fence or wall. Tying the stems to screws or wires attached to vine eyes is the easiest way to support them (p.222).

Creating contrast
A dark wall provides the perfect backdrop for the bright, creamy yellow blooms of 'Laura Ford'.

A charming climber
Clothing this stone wall is the climber 'Mary Wallace', making an eye-catching display in Les Jardins de Roquelin, a rose garden in the Loire Valley, France.

Arches

Arches work best when they serve a clear function in a garden: for instance, by marking the transition from one area to the next. They can be made out of wood or metal, and can be rustic, minimalist, or highly ornamental in style (although any ornamentation may well be hidden by the rose).

Metal arches don't rot and are available in a variety of finishes; powder-coated colours should last a long time. Wooden ones tend to have a limited life-span, especially if the base is sunk directly in the ground without a metal post base. Sweet chestnut, though, will last 40 years in the ground with no preservative. Whatever the material, an arch needs to be substantial to take the weight of the roses covering it, especially on a windy day. It needs to be at least 2.5m (8ft) high and 2m (6ft) wide, or it will be difficult to walk through without being attacked by the roses growing over it.

Choose varieties whose growth is relatively lax, or else they will send up vertical canes at the top that will look unattractive and be difficult to tie down. Many of the climbing English roses, as well as the patio climbers and ramblers, are particularly well-suited to arches, since they have the natural ability to flower more or less from the ground up – for example, 'Rambling Rosie' and 'Scent from Heaven'.

Blooming walkway
In Butchart Gardens, Victoria (British Colombia, Canada), a series of rose-covered arches create a vibrant walkway for visitors to enjoy.

Urban greenery
In this courtyard garden, 'Rambling Rector' blooms across steel girders, making the most of the light in this semi-shady space.

Pergolas

A pergola is effectively a series of joined-up arches that form an airy tunnel. It can be made entirely of wood, or more permanently by building brick or stone pillars and bridging them with horizontal timber beams. As with arches, the pergola needs to be high and wide enough that the roses don't obstruct the way through. And it is even more important that roses chosen to grow over a pergola have lax stems so that they can be easily trained horizontally: this generally means the ramblers. As most of these do not repeat-flower, a possible solution is to plant both a climber and a rambler at the base of each pillar: the former to clothe the vertical section and keep flowering later in the season, and the latter to grow up and over the top, its blooms hanging down gracefully. To encourage flowers right from the base of the pillar, circle the stems around the uprights at an angle of about 45 degrees.

Obelisks & pillars

Obelisks are useful for creating structure and adding height to a border. They also look good in winter when the roses grown up them are bare of flowers and leaves. They come in a wide range of shapes and sizes and it's particularly important to consider the height you'll need for your garden. If too short, the obelisk will be lost amongst the other plants growing around it. If too tall, it will dominate the border.

Obelisks are rather neat, geometrical shapes, and to show them off to best effect, anything grown up them needs to look in scale and not too out of control. This means that some of the more upright, taller shrubs, such as 'The Lady Gardener', 'Summer Memories', and 'The Ancient Mariner', are good options, rather than climbers or ramblers. To encourage as many flowers as possible and help limit the rose's height, circle its stems around the structure. Avoid choosing an over-vigorous rose: it's likely to overwhelm the obelisk and then look untidy.

Like obelisks, pillars can add height to a border, but take up less space at ground level. As they are usually no more than 10–15cm (4–6in) wide, circling a rose's stems round them is not easy. But, by spacing three or four pillars 20–30cm (8–12in) apart in a triangle or square, you can create more of a statement and make it easier to encircle the structure with roses. Pillars need roses of a suitable height, that can be kept tidy. Some of the shorter climbing and rambling English roses, as well as patio climbers and ramblers, will be good choices: for example, 'Lady of the Lake', 'Open Arms', and 'Rambling Rosie'.

Growing through trees

A rose-covered tree is a splendid sight, with flowers hanging down in large, fragrant garlands, and with the right choice, masses of small orange or red hips. Ramblers are usually a better choice than climbers as they are more likely to be able to compete successfully with the tree, and their lax growth will hang down more gracefully. Thorns come into their own in this situation, being the mechanism by which roses hang on to branches. While a thornless rambler might sound attractive, it is more likely to be blown out by the wind. The greater the number of thorns, and the more recurved they are, the better the rose will hang on.

It is important to match the vigour of the rose to the size of the tree: a super vigorous 8m (26ft) rambler such as 'Climbing Cécile Brunner' will be absolutely superb in a large tree like an oak or beech, but will quickly smother and kill a small or even medium-sized tree. The tree will eventually fall over, creating a magnificent rose heap – but this is only practical if you have a considerable amount of space.

For a medium-sized tree – say a birch, hazel, or an old apple – moderately vigorous ramblers like 'Adélaïde d'Orléans' and 'Francis E. Lester' that grow to about 5m (16ft) work well, allowing some of the supporting tree to show through. For a small tree like a hawthorn or a

"Ramblers are excellent for growing through trees: their flowers will hang down from branches in festoons."

cherry, varieties that grow only 2–4m (6–13ft) tall, such as pink 'Debutante' or 'Paul Noël' are perfect; the latter is also repeat-flowering, which is rare in ramblers.

Climbing companions

Rambling and climbing roses make wonderful supports for other climbers. There is a huge range of potential companions available in every conceivable size, but while a small climber can be grown up a large rose, the reverse (a *Clematis montana*, for example, growing up a 3m (10ft) climbing rose) would result in the rose being smothered.

The main choice is between using other climbers to extend the rose's season of interest (especially if, like most ramblers, it has just one glorious display in early summer) or going for planting partners whose flowers enhance each other. Clematis are perhaps the best climbers for

Clothing branches with blooms
In Yokohama Rose Garden, Japan, the large-flowering Pierre de Ronsard climbs up a tree, surrounded by a host of other varieties including Princess Alexandra of Kent, *R.* 'Sakurajima', *R.* 'Hiroshima-no-Kane', and *R.* 'Pēnelopeia'.

this purpose. They come in all different shapes and sizes, and it is possible to find one that flowers in every season, as well as a number that reliably repeat-flower over many months. 'Shimmer' is mid-purple to blue and grows to about 2m (6ft); 'Rebecca' grows to 2.5m (8ft) and has red flowers. Both flower from May to September. The late-flowering *Clematis viticella* varieties are always good with roses – for example, purple-pink 'Abundance', deep purple 'Black Prince', and white 'Alba Luxurians', which all grow to 3–4m (10–13ft).

Apricot delight
The climbing rose 'Crépuscule', with its apricot-yellow blooms, mingles here with the rich gold and plum shades of abutilon 'Orange Hot Lava' (California, USA).

"Enhance the beauty of your roses by juxtaposing them with contrasting plants."

For spring interest, the *Clematis macropetala* hybrids flower April to May and grow to about 3m (10ft) – for example, white 'Albina Plena' or violet 'Octopus'. Blue *Clematis alpina* 'Pamela Jackman' flowers a little earlier, from March to April. *Clematis rehderiana* and *C. tangutica* and its hybrids are more vigorous, and have yellow flowers from July to October. They look good growing up a rambler rose and have attractive seed heads.

Clematis do have an extensive root system which, when mature, will compete with that of the rose, so it may well be best to let the rose get established for two or three years before adding a clematis, or else planting it at least 1m (3ft) away.

Honeysuckles are another wonderful group of climbers, but many are so vigorous that they will easily smother a smaller rose. Some of the smaller ones are creamy yellow *Lonicera etrusca* 'Superba', red *L.* x *brownii* 'Dropmore Scarlet', and *L. periclymenum* 'Scentsation', all of which will flower around the same time as roses.

In mild areas with light frosts, *Sollya heterophylla*, with its small bright blue flowers would be effective. *Jasminum officinale* 'Devon Cream' or one of the star jasmines (*Trachelospermum* hybrids) add starry cream or white flowers and sweet perfume. Passionflower will twine through larger roses enthusiastically, adding an exotic touch.

Annual climbers can work really well with roses, as their root systems aren't as competitive as those of perennial ones. They also tend to have a longer flowering season. All can be grown from seed, or are available as young plants in the spring. Purple *Cobaea scandens* (cup-and-saucer vine) flowers until the end of autumn, and looks good next to roses with deep colours, such as rich apricot 'Lady of Shallot' or crimson 'Climbing Étoile de Hollande'.

Ipomoea purpurea (morning glory) has trumpet-shaped blue, red, pink, or purple flowers, which look dramatic twining through a bright pink rose like 'Gertrude Jekyll'. *Lathyrus odoratus* (sweet pea) is good, especially the old variety 'Cupani', which has the most superb fragrance. Its maroon and purple is an intriguing and vivid partner for the apricot and rose-pink of *Rosa* x *odorata* 'Mutabilis'. Sweet peas like plenty of moisture, so an occasional good soaking will help with their flowering.

For really tropical colours – perhaps to back some bright hybrid teas – *Thunbergia alata* (black-eyed Susan) has orange flowers with dark brown centres; there are varieties in other colours ranging from pink through yellow to cream.

Roses for autumn & winter

Long-flowering varieties, those with colourful autumn leaves and hips, and ornamental training of ramblers all offer interest during the dark months of the year.

The great majority of roses grown in gardens today will repeat-flower and, compared to most other plants, have an extremely long flowering season. They usually start up in early summer and, in temperate areas, finish in late autumn or early winter. Some though, with decent weather and a sheltered position, will carry on up to Christmas – and indeed may never stop. The tea roses are the main group to do this, although they do require a warm climate year-round to flourish. The Chinas too (especially *Rosa × odorata* 'Bengal Crimson' and 'Mutabilis') will carry on and on, and are not quite so fussy about it being warm the rest of the year. In climates whose "winter" is equivalent to a temperate season's summer, most repeat-flowering roses will produce their best flowers at that time, before taking their rest during the hot summer.

Some varieties have excellent autumn leaf colour, notably *R. spinosissima* 'Grandiflora', *R. virginiana*, *R. nitida* and *R. setigera*. *Rosa rugosa* leaves turn soft yellow, although only briefly before they drop.

Frosty elegance
In the grounds of Dunrobin Castle, Scotland, the near-bare stems of these climbing roses make an arresting winter sight across pyramid frames.

Winter beauty
As temperatures fall, the long-lasting blooms of 'Bonica' may be touched by frost.

Hips can provide winter colour (pp.158–63), as long as you choose those that last. Those on *Rosa sericea*, for example, drop quickly after colouring up. *Rosa rugosa* hips and some of the Chinese species like *R. moyesii* and *R. sweginzowii* look attractive until early winter, while others still look good well beyond midwinter. Because it's generally assumed that roses should be dead-headed, potential hip production is not recorded for many varieties. It's worth leaving the spent blooms on some to see what happens.

Mix hip-bearing roses with other shrubs with good autumn colour or berries, such as *Cornus sanguinea* 'Midwinter Fire', *Aucuba japonica* 'Crotonifolia', or *Skimmia japonica* 'Nymans'. Adding winter-flowerers like *Edgeworthia chrysantha*, *Lonicera fragrantissima*, or *Corylopsis pauciflora* will carry the interest through to the following spring.

The more vigorous ramblers can be trained in an ornamental way so that they look attractive between pruning and leafing out. Rather than cutting their long, flexible stems back, they are wound round in circles; this has the added advantage of encouraging more flowers. Climbers tend to be too stiff for this, and also resent having their stems facing downwards.

Tricky sites for roses

Not all gardens offer ideal conditions for roses due to lack of space, poor or no soil, extreme temperatures, or shade, but there are ways to work around these problems.

Poor soil

Most roses prefer a reasonably good, well-drained soil, although many will still grow well in less-than-ideal conditions with the addition of well-rotted organic matter (pp.208–209). If your soil is particularly shallow or fast-draining, it's worth trying tough varieties such as 'Bonica', *Rosa* x *alba* 'Alba Semiplena', or *Rosa* x *richardii*. On really sandy soils, species roses that grow wild along the coast like *Rosa rugosa* and *R. spinosissima* are the best choice. Their respective hybrids will do well too, as long as they are on their own roots or planted deeply enough to encourage rooting from the base of the stems.

While roses like a moist soil, the great majority will not grow well if their roots are wet for too long. The American species *Rosa palustris* and *R. californica*, both with rich-pink single flowers, are exceptions, having evolved to grow well in saturated soil. *R. virginiana* also flourishes in fairly wet soils, even those on the edge of salt marshes.

Using containers

If you can't plant them into good soil, you can grow roses successfully in large containers (pp.211–12). Terracotta or glazed pots offer better insulation for the roots than plastic, but you may still need to move pots into a sheltered spot, or wrap them in hessian or bubble wrap, if the temperature drops below −15°C (5°F), since plants in pots are more vulnerable than those in the ground.

Being raised up, with no competition or shading from the side, any rose grown in a container is likely to bush out sideways and create a more rounded shape. Still, it's best to start with a compact variety that has a fairly bushy habit, like 'Desdemona' or 'Fruity Parfuma', otherwise the upright stems will be very evident. Repeat-flowering and fragrance are desirable, if not essential requirements. Good disease-resistance is important, since the limited space of a pot can be quite stressful for the plant and make it more susceptible to diseases (although the greater airflow will help to ward them off). Many of the English roses are ideal, as are the floribundas (although fragrance is not their strong point). The smaller roses – miniatures, patios, and polyanthas – are also potential candidates, although fragrance is lacking in many of them. See pp.118–23 for more recommendations.

It's possible to grow shorter climbers and ramblers like 'Rambling Rosie' or 'Open Arms' in containers, and so be able to cover walls and fences. Some of the shorter "half" or "quarter" standard roses also work well, preferably with other plants such as *Erigeron karvinskianus* (Mexican fleabane) around their base.

Growing a rose in a pot makes it into a focal point, especially if it's a small variety that might otherwise get lost in a mixed bed. It's fun to group other pots around it, and experiment with different planting combinations. You can swap these around seasonally: for example, winter foliage plants such as *Bergenia purpurascens* var. *delavayi* or heuchera, followed by spring bulbs, and then summer perennials or bedding. In a really large container, you could even underplant the rose, perhaps with aubretia or *Phlox subulata* to trail over the edge.

Extreme temperatures

Gardens in the British Isles enjoy a temperate climate, where summers are rarely baking hot and winters are usually fairly mild. If you have a sunny coastal or urban garden, you will probably succeed with tea roses and be able to enjoy year-round flowers from Chinas. In places with really hot, dry summers, wild roses from places with a similar climate will thrive, such as the Mediterranean *R. gallica* and the Chinese *R. hugonis*.

Tolerance to winter cold differs greatly between varieties. Some, like the rugosas and other species native to northern areas, can withstand extreme cold down to −40°C (−40°F; RHS hardiness zone H7). The great majority of garden roses are fine with temperatures down to −10°C/14°F (RHS H4) or even −15°C/5°F (RHS H5).

Sharp drops in temperature, alternating with warm periods in late winter or early spring, are potentially damaging. If such cold spells are forecast, roses can be protected by leaning conifer branches against them. In more extreme conditions, wrapping hessian or piling up soil, straw, or leaves around the stems works well. Roses in containers are particularly susceptible to the cold, but can be brought inside an unheated garage or shed for the winter.

Tuscan sunshine
The Rose Garden at Borgo Santo Pietro, Italy, includes the white blooms of 'Winchester Cathedral' alongside the dark red roses of 'The Prince', with each bed framed with low box hedging.

Shady spots

When certain roses are recommended for shade, this does not mean that they will cope with no direct sunlight at all. Rather, these are varieties that need as little as four hours of direct sun a day – what most gardeners would consider "semi-shade" rather than shade. However, this does open up many more planting possibilities; especially in small town gardens that are inevitably shaded for part of the day by surrounding buildings or trees and where close planting means plants tend to shade each other. Roses can even be grown successfully against north-facing fences or walls, as long as they are not also shaded from the east or west.

As a general rule, once-flowering varieties like 'Alba Maxima', 'Ispahan', and 'Celsiana' cope better with shade than those that repeat-flower. Nevertheless, many of the latter will be fine, although because their leaves may stay wet for longer, disease may be more of an issue so it is important to choose varieties that are naturally very healthy, such as 'Olivia Rose Austin' and 'Joie de Vivre'.

Any variety that tends to send out long shoots may get drawn towards the light and be less successful in a shady spot. Sturdier, bushier varieties like 'Kew Gardens' and 'Bonica' will generally be better, especially if you want to grow roses under trees. A rambler, on the other hand, will be drawn up through the tree and eventually reach the sun.

Layers of interest
Featuring roses including 'Felicia', 'Munstead Wood', and 'Gertrude Jekyll', this mixed border is staggered across a series of dry stone walls to create height.

Inspired by nature

Many modern roses, as well as the species from which they are bred, have a wild feel to them and make great features in naturalistic planting schemes.

Wild gardens

Think of a romantic, overgrown cottage garden that mixes roses with old favourites such as peonies, delphiniums, and ox-eye daisies, or perhaps an archway or wall covered with a tangle of ramblers and honeysuckle, or a modern scheme that mixes ornamental grasses with large shrub roses. This is about letting your garden be a little wild and loose in style.

For a wild garden to work, all the plants in it need to have at least some semblance of wildness. The easiest way to achieve this is to plant wild roses (p.64), and the true species of any perennials and flowering shrubs you want to include. However, these can sometimes be difficult to source, very vigorous, and generally unruly. Wild roses, for example, are generally both tall and broad, often exceeding 2m (6ft) in both directions. For a smaller garden especially, the trick is to find garden hybrids that still look wild, and are attractive to wildlife, but which are much less aggressive, smaller, and will repeat-flower. Good roses that answer this description are 'Lupo', 'Ballerina', 'Morning Mist', 'Scented Carpet', 'Centre Stage', 'Scabrosa', and 'Fru Dagmar Hastrup'.

Roses with semi-double flowers would also work as long as they keep the informal, shrubby, often arching growth of the species, and aren't too brightly coloured. Some of the toughest are once-flowering varieties like *Rosa* x *alba* 'Alba Semiplena', 'Celsiana', *R. gallica* var. *officinalis* and *R. gallica* 'Versicolor' (*R. mundi*). Some repeat-flowering varieties would also be suitable, especially hybrid musks like 'Penelope', 'Vanity' (although perhaps a little on the bright side), and 'Trier', which all make substantial shrubs, or soft yellow 'Daybreak' and 'Callisto', which are much shorter.

Some of the English roses will fit in perfectly, such as 'Scarborough Fair', 'The Lady's Blush', 'Skylark' (with semi-double mid-pink flowers), and 'Comte de Champagne'. Other good modern varieties are 'Clair Martin', 'Île de Fleurs', and 'Pink Roadrunner'. All of these would look beautiful amongst other wild or wild-looking plants, but would need a little extra care and attention – they might well struggle if grasses and other plants were growing right round their base.

With enough space, you could allow a rambler to grow freely without any support to make a magnificent heap. The resulting arching growth would encourage even more flowers and, potentially, hips too. Before planting, clear the area of perennial weeds like thistles, nettles, bindweed, and docks (since extracting them later from a mass of rose stems would be unpleasant). To encourage a little more height, erect a 1.5–2m (5–6ft) triangular or square support for the stems to grow through and arch over. Some suitable varieties would be 'Francis E. Lester', 'Adélaïde d'Orléans', 'Rambling Rector', 'Polyantha Grandiflora', and the less vigorous (and repeat-flowering) 'The Lady of the Lake' and 'Open Arms'.

Meadows with roses

Roses make a great addition to planting schemes inspired by natural meadows, used either as boundary hedges (pp.34–35) or to make hummocks or heaps – as they often do naturally in mountain hay meadows. The competition from meadow grasses can benefit species roses by curbing their

A meadow pairing
The soft yellow blooms of 'Tottering-by-Gently' can be seen here mingling with ox-eye daisies.

Wilder by nature
The large, arching growth of *Rosa* 'Cerise Bouquet' makes a stunning addition to this wildflower meadow in Rockcliffe Garden, Gloucestershire.

exuberant growth and giving them a more natural look. They will also be more likely to set a good crop of hips and develop autumn colour on their leaves.

It's important to match the potential size of the rose with that of the meadow. If space is limited – say, less than 5m² (55ft²) – short, compact species like *Rosa spinosissima*, *R. nitida*, and *R. gallica* are good choices. If there's a bit more room, try *Rosa rugosa*, *R. palustris*, *R. virginiana*, or *R. woodsii*. Bigger meadows offer the widest choice, including some yellow roses, such as *Rosa xanthina* f. *hugonis*, *R. ecae*, and *R. primula*. Added to these are some excellent near-wild hybrids, including *R. xanthina* 'Canary Bird', 'Cantabrigiensis', and 'Headleyensis'.

There are also many large species roses in white, pink, and red to choose from. Probably the best known and most garden-worthy is 'Geranium', a hybrid of *Rosa moyesii* with bright red flowers and scarlet, flagon-shaped hips. *Rosa setipoda* and *R. sweginzowii* are similar, with generous quantities of paler pink flowers. While the hips of these are very showy, they aren't particularly long-lasting, as they tend to lose their colour and plumpness in early winter. Also from China: free-flowering, tough, reliable, and with a good crop of hips are *R. davidii* and *R. multibracteata*. A special mention should be made of a particular form of *R. sericea* – *pteracantha*, which has very large, flattened, bright red thorns that look dramatic when the sun is shining through them. It needs pruning hard each year, since these thorns only appear on young stems. *R. roxburghii* has showy flowers and hips, and makes a fine shrub.

A number of North American and European species make fine large shrubs in a meadow setting. The flowers are all various shades of pink and their hips are generally longer lasting than the Chinese species – sometimes lasting right through the winter. *R. californica* and *R. nutkana* come from North America, while *R. villosa*, *R. rubiginosa*, and *R. canina* are native to Europe. There are also a number of excellent species hybrids that retain that wild look and are happy growing in grass: *R.* x *hibernica* from *R. canina*, 'Scarlet Fire' from *R. gallica*, and the Frühlings series, including 'Frühlingsgold', from *R. spinosissima*.

Many garden roses with single or semi-double, wild-looking flowers would also work. *Rosa* x *alba* 'Alba Semiplena', an extraordinarily tough and adaptable rose, is one of the best. 'Violacea' has good-sized, striking, deep-purple blooms, although sadly no hips. 'Complicata' is much more modern, first appearing in the early 20th century, but looks perfectly at home in wild areas, the pink flowers being followed by large, rounded hips. Of the repeat-flowering roses, 'Topolina', 'Tottering-By-Gently', and 'The Lady's Blush' would all fit in well and be tough enough to cope with the conditions, although they might need a bit more care and attention – for example, keeping the space immediately round their base clear and mulched.

Roses for wildlife

With their long flowering season, and hips in the autumn and winter, roses are some of the best plants to support the type of wildlife that most of us want to attract to our gardens, like bees, hoverflies, small mammals, and birds.

A great variety of insects are fond of visiting the flowers of roses. While they lack nectar, their pollen is highly nutritious: rich in proteins, amino acids, carbohydrates, lipids, and vitamins. Bees – honey, carpenter, and bumble – take this back to their nests to feed their larvae, while other insects – including hoverflies and beetles – eat it while on the flower.

It's easy to assess the potential value to pollinators of a semi-double or double rose by gently parting its petals and looking into the centre: if there is a good boss of stamens, there is a good chance the pollen will be collected or eaten. Many insects are willing to wheedle their way in through tight spaces if they think the effort will be worthwhile. The flowers of 'Lady of Shalott', for example, are not too double and their stamens are still easily

A winter feast
The red hips of the dog rose, *Rosa canina*, offer a vital food source for birds over the winter months, when other food sources are scarce.

accessible. In very full blooms, the stamens are transformed into small petals, and so are of no value to insects. Avoid these varieties if your aim is to attract and support wildlife.

Rose hips are hugely valuable to wildlife. They come in a huge variety of different shapes, sizes, and colours, and while some only last a few weeks once ripe, others stay attached through winter, meaning you can offer a supply of hips from midsummer (*R. sericea* and *R. fedtschenkoana*) to the following spring ('Grouse', 'Partridge', and 'Polyantha Grandiflora'). 'Bonica' and 'The Generous Gardener' are unusual in having more double flowers as well as setting a good crop of hips. Siting a rose that keeps its hips through the winter near the house will give you a good view of the birds that come to eat them.

Species roses and ramblers, with their open flowers and abundance of hips, offer the best of both worlds when it comes to supporting wildlife. Ramblers, in particular, can't be beaten in terms of sheer numbers of flowers and hips. On a mature plant of *Rosa filipes* 'Kiftsgate' or 'Francis E. Lester', there will be many, many thousands of flowers followed by a similar number of hips. These are of particular value to birds, since many are just the right size to be picked off one by one and to slip nicely down the gullet, while the mature ramblers' size will provide safety for the birds, since they can perch high above the ground. *Rosa rugosa* and some of its hybrids produce a great crop of lovely, large, juicy, and presumably tasty hips that birds and small mammals relish.

Bee-friendly blooms
The open flowers of the rambler 'Goldfinch' make it easy for bumblebees to access their pollen.

Winter bounty
The scarlet hips of *Rosa rubiginosa,* shown here alongside the darker red hawthorn berries and ripening blackberries, provide a valuable food source to birds through the autumn and winter months.

All hips not eaten on the branch will eventually drop off or be removed when the rose is pruned. Leave them on the ground: there, they'll become a good source of food for ground-dwelling creatures, whether mammals or invertebrates, or else will be broken down into organic matter by fungi and soil-dwellers – if they don't develop into seedlings, that is.

A successful wildlife garden will offer plenty of shelter for all kinds of mammals, birds, and insects. In a small space, aim for a tangle of roses on boundary fences – perhaps be freer in how you prune them, so they bush out a little. Or even better, plant a mixed hedge that includes wild-looking roses such as *R. rubiginosa* or *R. glauca* mixed with other shrubs and climbers attractive to wildlife, such as honeysuckle, blackthorn, hawthorn, and field maple. If you have space, a thicket or hummock of roses (p.53) will also be a valuable habitat.

Apart from insects that collect and eat their pollen and assorted creatures that eat their hips, roses are beloved by a huge array of seemingly less attractive visitors: aphids that suck their sap; bees, beetles, and caterpillars that eat their leaves; and occasionally insects that bore into their stems. While these all harm roses, they're also food for other creatures. Aphids are a classic example that can multiply at a frightening pace, but a healthy population of beneficial insects and birds will happily keep them in check. The aphids are an important part of the garden ecosystem, which is why it is so important that, unless absolutely necessary, they are not controlled artificially using insecticides or any other means.

"Look out for signs of the leafcutter bee: its beautifully excised leaf cuts should be admired."

ROSE

types

The evolution of garden roses

Most of the development of the huge range of flower-forms, colours, growth habits, and scents in the roses available today has happened in the last 200 years.

Plants started appearing about 500 million years ago, but fossils found in Asia suggest that it wasn't until the Eocene period, about 35 million years ago, that roses first evolved. Other fossils found in Colorado and Oregon have been identified as being possibly *Rosa nutkana* and *R. palustris*, both still common in North America. Today there are estimated to be about 150 species of wild roses, but only eight of them have been widely used in the development of the many thousands of garden roses that have been introduced.

Initially, any new roses would have been the result of chance crosses that appeared in gardens, or mutations of existing roses. During the 18th and early 19th centuries, rose breeders developed large-scale breeding programmes, comparable to the breeders of today, who grow over 100,000 seedlings each year. However, all of their plants would have been the chance crosses produced by the natural inclination of bees as they visited flowers in succession. It wasn't until towards the middle of the 19th century that specific varieties were crossed with the idea of a certain goal in mind. English nurseryman William Paul was one of the early rose breeders, although one gets the impression that he regarded the whole process as a bit too fiddly and long-winded, since after a time he gave up noting parents.

This new, more scientific approach really took off with François Lacharme of Lyon (whose only well-known rose today is 'Madame Plantier', p.175) and Englishman Henry Bennett (whose best-known rose is 'Mrs John Laing'). The latter was a cattle farmer from Wiltshire who was familiar with strict breeding programmes designed to produce better offspring. He

Living history
These three varieties show the characteristics of roses through the ages, from a near-species hybrid (left), through an early modern hybrid (centre), to a modern hybrid (right).

Rosa gallica var. *officinalis*

'Président de Sèze'

'Royal William'

Diversity of form
Standard, rambler, and shrub roses in the gardens of Mottisfont Abbey, UK.

set up state-of-the-art facilities with heated greenhouses, and in 1879 introduced ten "Pedigree Hybrids of the Tea Rose", which in 1890 were renamed "hybrid teas". (Although the parents aren't known for sure, the first generally recognized hybrid tea, 'La France', was bred by Jean-Baptiste Guillot (Fils) and introduced in 1867.)

Since then, the breeding of roses has become very sophisticated, although the same basic process is used in most cases: a knife or scissors to harvest the stamens and a paint brush to apply the pollen. A computer has become invaluable for determining the best parents and crosses. Each year the biggest breeders make over 100,000 crosses, using over 100 different parents to produce several hundred thousand seeds. The resulting seedlings are then trialled for several years before the final decision is made as to which to introduce. The whole process usually takes ten years from crossing to introduction. Careful record-taking at each stage is crucial to producing better varieties. The chances of creating something better and significantly different than either of the parents is extremely small, and when a promising new rose is identified, it has to be increased in number from the initial one to the many plants needed to introduce it to the world.

Species roses & their hybrids

Wild roses have the simplest flowers. They are full of character and thrive in a wide range of situations, although most need space to do their best.

Roses are only native to regions north of the equator, from North America across Europe, North Africa, the Middle East to Asia. There are about 150 species, mostly in Asia (the variations within each species and their readiness to hybridize with each other makes counting them difficult). The dog rose, *Rosa canina*, for example, can reproduce asexually and so botanists disagree as to whether to treat it as one species or a huge number of different ones.

The great majority of wild roses are various shades of pink or white, with a few reds and yellows. With the exception of the *Rosa sericea* group which have four, all of them have five petals. Fragrance is very variable in strength and type, as is habit and height, with *Rosa spinosissima* being one of the shortest, only about 15cm (6in) tall when growing on sand dunes and exposed to strong winds. By contrast, some of the big climbing species native to warm parts of Asia can reach 15m (50ft) to the top of large trees.

Most species roses only flower once in a season. The exceptions include *R. rugosa*, *R. bracteata*, and *R. fedtschenkoana*. Wild rose hips are very variable in size, shape, and colour. Some stay attached for many months, while others drop off almost as soon as they are ripe.

A number of wild roses are very garden-worthy – for example, *R. moyesii*, *R. roxburghii*, and *R. glauca* – and look superb growing in long grass or up into trees. They need little or no maintenance and shouldn't be pruned at all. All, of course, are excellent for wildlife, providing pollen, fruit, and safe shelter in their thorny thickets.

Rosa glauca

Rosa bracteata

R. × cantabrigiensis (yellow blooms, left) accompanied by topiary balls and surrounded by cow parsley and forget-me-nots

Rugosas

One of the most useful species roses, *Rosa rugosa* is native to the coasts of northern Japan, North Korea, northeastern China, and Siberia, and so is incredibly winter hardy and tolerant of salt-laden winds. It is also free of disease and able to cope with poor soils. Its fragrance is strong and exactly like that of the old roses. It also has the ability – rare in wild roses – of being able to repeat-flower, the flowers being followed by large hips. It is not surprising that it has been used extensively in breeding programmes.

The best of its hybrids are as healthy and winter hardy as their parent, grow well in hot or cooler summers, and have flowers varying from single to fully double. The great majority are various shades of pink, white, and purple, with some of the best being 'Hansa', 'Roseraie de l'Haÿ', and 'Blanche Double de Coubert'. There are a few in shades of apricot and yellow, such as Agnes. Some still bear the large hips of the species. Unfortunately, some varieties are not as resistant to disease, especially rust, as *Rosa rugosa*. Most are large shrubs, 2m (6ft) or more, but recently some short shrubs, less than 1m (3ft) tall, have been introduced.

'Roseraie de l'Haÿ'

Rosa spinosissima 'William III'

Spinosissimas

Rosa spinosissima is an extremely tough rose native from Iceland across Europe and Asia, and even into North Africa. It has many synonyms, most commonly *R. pimpinellifolia*, and is also known as the Scotch or burnet rose. It is often seen growing by the sea, where it grows no more than 15cm (6in) tall, although in better conditions it reaches 1m (3ft). It is thorny, with small leaves. The small white flowers are produced early, have a lovely lily-of-the-valley fragrance, and are followed by round black hips and often a superb display of autumn colour on the leaves.

During the first half of the 19th century, hundreds of forms and hybrids were selected and introduced. While nearly all have small flowers, they vary in number of petals from five (the very beautiful 'Dunwich Rose', see p.131) to a few tens (the double, white-flowered form), and in colour from white through all shades of pink ('Andrewsii') to purple ('William III') as well as yellow (*R.* × *harrisonii* 'Williams' Double Yellow'). Some are bicoloured with a different colour on the reverse ('Single Cherry', see p.138) or two shades on each petal ('Marbled Pink').

None of these older varieties repeat-flower except 'Stanwell Perpetual', a lovely rose with large, very double, strongly scented blooms. More recently new interest in the spinosissimas has resulted in some repeat-flowering varieties being introduced such as 'Silas Marner' and 'Peter Boyd', named after the world authority on them.

"An incredibly tough rose, *R. spinosissima* can be found growing on sand dunes in the wild."

The oldest garden roses

These roses have one flush of many-petalled flowers each year. Most have an "old rose" fragrance – the rich scent that's most associated with roses.

Gallicas

The gallicas are the oldest of the garden roses. They originated from *Rosa gallica*, a short, suckering rose native to southern and central Europe, with pale pink to red flowers and often a strong, delicious fragrance. Its hybrids are characterized by dark foliage, the almost complete absence of thorns, and flowers mostly in shades of mid-pink to purple, with a number having striped petals. Many have a wonderfully rich fragrance.

The oldest of the gallicas and thus, most probably, of cultivated roses is *R. gallica* var. *officinalis*, which may date back to Roman times. It became hugely important in France from the Middle Ages, being grown in great quantities for its medicinal, culinary, and cosmetic properties. *Rosa gallica* 'Versicolor' (also known as *R. mundi*) is a striped sport (spontaneous genetic mutation) dating from the 16th century.

Most gallicas were bred in the 19th century in France, some of the better ones being 'Tuscany Superb', 'Charles de Mills', 'Président de Sèze', and 'Ipsilanté'. They are generally tough, reliable, and easy to grow. They are effective in mixed borders, but some can sucker freely.

'Charles de Mills'

'Celsiana'

Damasks

The damasks, like the gallicas and albas, are an ancient group, all once-flowering with one intriguing exception. They are usually quite easy to distinguish from the gallicas with their rather laxer growth, pricklier stems, paler green leaves, and white or paler pink flowers. They are typically more strongly and deliciously fragrant than the gallicas, too: it is from a group of damasks (collectively called 'Kazanlik') that the essential oil attar of roses is distilled.

Their origin is a bit of a mystery. DNA analysis suggests that they are a product of three parents: *Rosa gallica*, *R. moschata*, and *R. fedtschenkoana*. Pollen from *R. gallica* fertilized the ovule of *R. moschata* to produce a hybrid rose, which in turn acted as a seed parent, using pollen from *R. fedtschenkoana*. While roses generally happily cross with each other, how did these three get together in the first place? They do not naturally grow in the same areas. Perhaps it all happened in someone's garden.

'Quatre Saisons' (p.150) is the only old rose to repeat-flower, and is possibly the same long-flowering rose that we are told was growing in ancient Greek and Roman times (pp.8–11). There are also a number of wonderful once-flowering damasks, including 'Madame Hardy', 'Ispahan', and 'Celsiana'.

"Of an estimated 150 wild rose species, only eight have been widely used to develop the garden roses we see today."

Rosa x *alba* 'Alba Semiplena'

Albas

Albas are perhaps the most distinct of the three most ancient types of roses, with grey-green leaves, sturdy, upright growth, and white or pale pink flowers. Many of them have superb fragrance. *Rosa* x *alba* 'Alba Semiplena' is probably also one of the earliest roses to have been cultivated in gardens, possibly as far back as Roman times – no doubt for its excellent crop of hips as well as its beautiful blooms and exquisite scent.

DNA analysis indicates that albas are crosses between varieties of *Rosa gallica* and *R. canina*. They are a tough group, able to survive poor conditions and years of neglect. They are some of the best roses for shady positions and look lovely mixed in with other plants. Most varieties were bred in the 19th century, with some of the best being 'Alba Maxima', 'Königin von Dänemark', and 'Great Maiden's Blush'.

Centifolias

The centifolias are perhaps the least garden-worthy of the once-flowering old roses. Their growth is often difficult to manage, their flowers are a little too heavy, and their health not great. But of course, there are exceptions, and both *Rosa* x *centifolia* (the original variety) and 'Fantin-Latour' have beautiful flowers. Fragrance is variable, but very good in some.

Centifolias date back to the late 16th century, and are probably the result of a cross made in Holland between various gallicas and damasks. The original centifolia often features in Dutch and Flemish flower paintings. It is rather unkindly known as the cabbage rose, although old herbalists called it the queen of roses. A number of centifolias are unusual sports – some dwarfs (*R.* x *centifolia* 'De Meaux'), one with a flower bud like Napoleon's hat (*R.* x *c.* 'Cristata', or 'Chapeau de Napoléon'), and – most famously – moss roses.

'Fantin-Latour'

Mosses

These roses are characterized by mossy growth around their flower buds and in some cases down their stems. It feels sticky when rubbed, and has a delicious, resinous smell. This moss was found originally on sports in the damask and centifolia groups of roses; the former producing brown moss, the latter green moss. It was first spotted in the middle of the 17th century in France, probably on the rose we now call *Rosa* x *centifolia* 'Muscosa' or 'Old Pink Moss'. It wasn't until the middle of the 19th century that breeders, particularly Philippe-Victor Verdier in France, developed new varieties. The Victorians loved them.

As might be expected from their parentage – both damasks and centifolias – the mosses are a mixed group of roses. They are nearly all once-flowering but a few, resulting from crosses with Chinas (p.72), repeat-flower well ('Mousseline' is the best). Unfortunately, mosses aren't especially disease-resistant. Most are shades of pink, a few being white, purple, or striped. The darkest is the upright and short 'Nuits de Young' (p.113). 'William Lobb' (p.161) is rather paler and extremely vigorous; it can be grown as a climber. Its crimson-purple flowers fade to lavender and eventually almost grey.

'William Lobb'

Repeat-flowering old roses

These roses all have their origins in China, and some flower throughout the season. The colours include apricot and yellow, and there is a wide variety of fragrances.

Chinas

The Chinese had been growing and breeding roses for a very long time before any of their varieties were exported to the West. 'Old Blush China' (also known as 'Parson's Pink', and now as *Rosa* × *odorata* 'Pallida'), for example, had been grown in China and possibly Japan for at least a thousand years, valued for its continuous flowering. It was one of the first two Chinas to come to Europe, probably in the middle of the 18th century, the other being 'Slater's Crimson' (now *R. chinensis* 'Semperflorens'). These were followed by *R.* × *odorata* 'Hume's Blush Tea-scented China' in 1809, and finally 'Parks' Yellow China' in 1824.

More Chinas were developed from these initial introductions, mostly in France. As a group they are characterized by light, airy growth and single, semi-double, or loosely double flowers, mostly in shades of white, pink, and red; although, for the first time in hybrid roses, we see some soft yellow and apricot colours in *R.* × *odorata* 'Mutabilis' and 'Comtesse du Cayla'.

Given a warm position, some of the Chinas will flower all year round, as does *R.* × *odorata* 'Bengal Crimson' in the Chelsea Physic Garden in London.

R. × *odorata* 'Mutabilis'

'Louise Odier'

Bourbons

A few years after Chinese roses first reached Europe, on the Île de Bourbon (now known as Réunion) in the Indian Ocean, colonial farmers grew 'Old Blush China' and 'Quatre Saisons' side by side in hedges. A different-looking seedling appeared close by and was spotted by a Monsieur Perichon. Seeds from it were sent back to France, and the resulting rose was much admired for its rich pink blooms and ability to repeat-flower. It was introduced in 1823 under the name of 'Le Rosier de l'Île de Bourbon'.

This rose was passed around, new varieties were swiftly bred from it, and so the Bourbon roses were born. Nearly all are pink, a few red or white, and several striped. Most have strongly fragrant, many-petalled flowers very much in the style of the old roses, but you can see the beginnings of modern roses in their leaves and stems, which look like those of the hybrid teas. Almost all of them repeat-flower. Unfortunately they are quite susceptible to blackspot, powdery mildew, and rust. The flowers of most varieties also spoil badly in the rain. 'Louise Odier' and 'Madame Isaac Péreire' are perhaps the two best.

'Portlandica'

'Ferdinand Pichard'

Portlands

The Portlands are a relatively small but select group, well worth a place in the garden for their beauty, fragrance, repeat-flowering, and general health. The original Portland rose (also known as 'Portlandica', 'Paestana', or 'Portland Crimson Monthly Rose') dates back to at least 1783. It repeat-flowers, has dark pink or pale crimson semi-double flowers, and was probably a cross between *Rosa gallica* var. *officinalis* and 'Quatre Saisons'.

Portlands are much more upright and sturdy in habit than damasks, with short flower stems. They are perfect for mixing in with other plants, in formal settings, or even as a hedge. Most are pink but there are some very dark ones like 'Indigo', while 'Marbrée' has deep purple flowers mottled with paler pink. There are three particularly garden-worthy ones: 'Jacques Cartier' (p.144), 'Comte de Chambord' (p.97), and 'Rose de Rescht' (p.144).

Hybrid perpetuals

The hybrid perpetuals are the result of crossing various roses from a wide variety of groups including Portlands, hybrid Chinas, and Bourbons. Many were introduced in the late 19th century, when flower shows were popular and the ideal in a rose to exhibit was the perfection of its bud. Most breeders were intent on perfecting the beauty and shape of the flowers with little regard for the overall shape of the plant or its health – they thought nothing of using extremely toxic pesticides to keep their roses free of pests and diseases. As a result, many of the varieties are rather coarse shrubs or climbers, with poor disease resistance.

The flowers are all shades of white, pink, and red. 'Ferdinand Pichard' is striped pink and red, and 'Roger Lambelin' red splashed with white. The strongly fragrant 'Souvenir du Docteur Jamain' is a wonderfully rich dark crimson but doesn't flower freely and makes a sparse, lanky climber. 'Paul Neyron' boasts some of the largest flowers to be found in the rose world. 'Reine des Violettes', 'Duke of Edinburgh', and 'Ferdinand Pichard' are perhaps the three best.

Tea roses

The tea roses are the result of crossing *Rosa × odorata* 'Hume's Blush Tea-scented China' and 'Parks' Yellow China' with various Bourbons and noisettes, the first – 'Adam' – being introduced in 1835. The flowers have a delicate charm in which one can see the beginnings of the hybrid tea bloom with its high, pointed centre. Those that are very double (like 'Maman Cochet' and 'Devoniensis') open up to look much like the old roses, with beautifully arranged petals. They were originally called "tea-scented China roses", since they smelled like a freshly opened packet of China tea. This scent may be mixed with a wide range of others, including violet, freesia, carnation, citrus, banana, and camphor.

Tea roses vary greatly in colour and include for the first time in hybrid roses a true, rich yellow ('Perle des Jardins') and apricot ('Lady Hillingdon' – see p.174 for the climbing version). They vary greatly in size, too, from small bushes to tall climbers, although their eventual height is much affected by climate and soil. They love the heat, and flower nearly all year round in warm places. In the cooler climate of the UK they are much less satisfactory, and struggle to grow and flower.

Polyanthas

The polyanthas are not a well-known group but they do include some pretty, garden-worthy varieties. Typically they have small, double, white or pink flowers on a short, quite compact shrub. Their common parent is *Rosa multiflora* (formerly known as *R. polyantha*) – a vigorous rambler with small white fragrant flowers that is happy to cross with most other roses, seeding itself around with gay abandon. The first recognized polyantha, 'Pâquerette', was introduced in 1875 by Jean-Baptiste Guillot (Fils), and probably has 'Old Blush China' in its background.

Those in vivid colours include the 'Orléans Rose', with open cherry-red, white-centred flowers. This produced many sports, including crimson 'Miss Edith Cavell' (p.126), and has also been important in the breeding of nearly all polyanthas and floribundas. Other brightly coloured polyanthas include orange-scarlet 'Paul Crampel' and purple 'Baby Faurax'.

Most polyanthas have no fragrance, but there are exceptions, such as 'Marie Pavié' (p.123). The best known polyantha is 'Cécile Brunner' (p.200), whose pink flower buds are like those on a perfect miniature hybrid tea. All polyanthas repeat-flower well and will associate beautifully with other plants in mixed borders.

'Climbing Lady Hillingdon'

'Cécile Brunner'

Modern roses

From the middle of the 19th century, scientific breeding methods produced a wider range of colours and forms in roses, and repeat-flowering became common.

Hybrid teas

Originally these were the result of crosses between a tea rose (for the flower form) and a hybrid perpetual (for vigour) in the 1860s. The early varieties were beautiful at both the bud and open flower stages, and their growth was quite bushy; but breeders focused purely on making the buds more classically beautiful, with a high, pointed centre. The fully open flowers of the new varieties often lacked definition and were not particularly attractive.

Hybrid teas were a plant of their time, with their bright colours, suitability for mass planting, and – as pesticides were widely used with impunity – less than perfect health. As tastes changed and gardeners demanded roses with good disease resistance, they fell out of favour. The most famous hybrid tea is 'Peace', introduced in 1945, and partly responsible for the huge boost in popularity of roses in the 1940s and 50s. It is in the background of great numbers of subsequent varieties. 'Warm Wishes', with its high-pointed centre and perfectly arranged outer petals, is another classic example.

'Warm Wishes'

'Iceberg'

Floribundas

The breeders who developed the floribundas were looking for a mass of colour on a tough, winter-hardy bush. The form of the flower and the fragrance were less important. The first varieties were bred by D. T. Poulsen in Denmark, who crossed polyanthas with hybrid teas. He introduced 'Red Riding Hood' (or 'Rödhätte') in 1912, but it wasn't until after the First World War that other breeders around the world joined in and floribundas (known at first as hybrid polyanthas) became popular. As tastes changed, the individual flowers became more hybrid tea-like.

'Iceberg' is easily the most famous of the floribundas (even though, strictly speaking, it's actually a hybrid musk). 'Trumpeter' is a classic 1970s floribunda, with loosely double flowers of an almost fluorescent orange-red.

Low-growing beauty
Vivid pink patio roses soften the edge of this paved limestone path.

"While a small rose variety can get lost in a mixed bed, if planted into a container, it becomes a true focal point."

Patio roses

Patio roses – also known as minifloras and dwarf cluster-flowered – are somewhere between floribundas and miniature roses: about 60cm (2ft) tall, with flowers about 5cm (2in) across. Both plant and flower size are intermediate. They flower freely and are useful for the edge of a border or for containers. They come from a very mixed background, and so the flowers vary greatly in number of petals and colour. 'Queen Mother' is one of the best known, with soft pink semi-double flowers. 'Sweet Dream' has very full peach-coloured flowers, and 'Marlena' is semi-double and scarlet.

Miniature roses

These are the smallest roses, usually less than 60cm (2ft) tall, with flowers that are only about 2.5cm (1in) across. While they can be grown in the ground, they are ideal for containers, where it is easier to appreciate their often pretty flowers, some of them perfect old rose-style rosettes. The original miniature roses probably came from China around 1800. A number of varieties were bred, but they didn't become popular until in 1918, when a perpetual-flowering dwarf rose was found in Switzerland and named 'Rouletii'. Soon, many new varieties bred from it – including 'Para Ti' (also known as 'Pour Toi') by Pedro Dot in Spain.

The remarkable Californian rose breeder Ralph Moore introduced many miniatures, including 'Stars 'n' Stripes' and 'Little Flirt', in the second half of the 20th century. In Europe, they are mostly seen as pot plants, bought as a colourful, but perhaps short-lived, present. Poulsen Roses of Denmark developed varieties that can be grown easily from cuttings, flower 12 months of the year, and withstand the rigours of being transported long distances in lorries.

'Pour Toi'

79

Hybrid musks

Most hybrid musks have small to medium-sized flowers in large sprays in shades of white, pink, yellow, or buff with a fruity, musky fragrance. The best-known ones – 'Penelope', 'Cornelia', 'Felicia', and 'Buff Beauty' – make large shrubs at least 2m (6ft) tall and across, and which in warm climates can make substantial climbers.

In the early 20th century the Reverend Joseph Pemberton, a keen exhibitor of the rather fussy hybrid perpetuals (p.74), decided to try and breed roses that would be tougher and easier to grow. He started with 'Trier', a large shrub with fragrant, small, nearly single white flowers, as well as various polyanthas, hybrid teas, teas, and noisettes. The first three varieties above were bred by him. More recently, Louis Lens in Belgium used dwarf *Rosa multiflora* and *R. helenae* hybrids to produce short, repeat-flowering, hardy shrubs and ramblers such as 'Guirlande d'Amour' (p.197) and 'Sibelius' (p.121). His successors, Rudy and Ann Velle, have produced some lovely, scented, healthy varieties including 'Caroline's Heart' and 'Fil des Saisons'.

Must-have hybrid musk
The soft apricot buds and white blooms of 'Penelope' (right) are paired with the brighter apricot 'Just Joey' beneath two pleached lime trees.

'Rosy Cushion'

Modern shrub roses

This group encompasses a wide range of varieties bred in the 20th and 21st centuries, originally arising from crosses of various species roses with hybrid teas and floribundas. There is no common denominator to them: flower size ranges from small to very large, number of petals from 5 to over 100, and fragrance from none to strong. Some are short, others tall; some repeat-flower, while others don't. In general, though, they are tough roses that grow well in less than ideal conditions.

More recently, modern shrub roses have improved greatly and many make good garden plants. 'Frühlingsgold', 'Nevada', and 'Rosy Cushion' are good older varieties. The German breeders Kordes have been responsible for many excellent recent varieties, such as 'Lemon Fizz', 'Summer Memories' and 'Île de Fleurs'. Mention must also be made of the Knock Out series bred by Bill Radler in the US. The original 'Knock Out' was introduced in 2000 and many millions have been sold in North America. It has been followed by a number of others, including 'Pink Knock Out', 'Double Knock Out', and 'Sunny Knock Out'.

'Gertrude Jekyll'

English roses

The English roses were developed by British breeder David Austin, his ambition being to create varieties that had the charm and fragrance of old roses combined with the repeat-flowering and wide colour range of modern roses. He started by crossing old roses with various hybrid teas and floribundas, which led to a small group of once-flowering roses including his first well-known variety, 'Constance Spry' (p.146), in 1961.

Austin's roses slowly became better known and received a big boost in 1983 when he introduced three varieties at the Chelsea Flower Show: 'Mary Rose', 'Heritage', and the one most responsible for English roses becoming well known, not only in the UK but also in North America, Europe, and Australasia, 'Graham Thomas' (p.193).

'Gertrude Jekyll', with its very strong, old rose fragrance, was introduced in 1986, while newer varieties include 'Roald Dahl' (p.90), 'Gabriel Oak' (p.100), 'Eustacia Vye' (p.109), and 'Desdemona' (p.109, p.123). These have become extremely popular around the world due to their overall beauty, fragrance, and, increasingly, their health. There are a number of climbers and repeat-flowering ramblers among the English roses.

Ground-cover roses

These ground-hugging roses are usually no more than 50cm (18in) tall and very variable in how far they spread. They form a thick mat that supposedly prevents weeds growing through them. Weeds, though, are not easily deterred, and they will soon grow through, giving you the unpleasant job of extracting them from between thorny stems.

Ground-cover roses are perhaps better seen as free-flowering, short-growing, mound-forming roses, suitable for the edge of a border or path, or for growing in a container where they will trail attractively over the rim. All have small flowers, usually produced continuously over a long season. Some, such as 'Grouse', 'Partridge', and 'Alexander von Humboldt', will produce an excellent crop of hips. Most have little or no scent, but some good exceptions are 'Centre Stage', 'Scented Carpet', 'Grouse', and 'Partridge'. When the first of the Flower Carpet series was introduced in 1989, it attracted much attention for its bright pink flowers and excellent health, as well as for the bright pink pot it was sold in. Its breeder, Noack of Germany, has since introduced a number of others in different colours, with 'Flower Carpet White' being perhaps the best.

'White Flower Carpet'

Climbing roses

This is a very variable group of roses, coming from a great mix of parentages, all having the propensity to climb, but varying in height, stiffness, and ability to repeat-flower.

'Blush Noisette'

'Climbing Madame Caroline Testout'

Noisettes

These are some of the most beautiful climbers for a warmer, Mediterranean climate. The first of them, a cross between the vigorous climbing species *Rosa moschata* and 'Old Blush China', was called 'Champney's Pink Cluster'. This was probably a chance seedling that grew in John Champney's garden in South Carolina in the early 1800s. A local nurseryman, Philippe Noisette, collected seed from it and grew a shorter, continuously flowering rose that he named 'Blush Noisette'. The flowers of most varieties bred from this are loosely or fully double, medium to large, come in a wide range of colours, and often have a lovely fragrance. A number of them, like 'Rêve d'Or' and 'Crépuscule', are yellow or apricot, achieved by crossing 'Blush Noisette' with 'Parks' Yellow China'.

'Madame Alfred Carrière' (p.176) is probably both the best known and hardiest of the noisettes: it has highly fragrant, large, cupped, blush-pink flowers and is very vigorous, needing plenty of space.

Climbers

While a climbing rose is easy to define – a rose that grows to a height of between say 2m (6ft) and 10m (33ft) – the propensity of a variety to climb will depend very much on the climate and how it is pruned. A shrub in a cooler climate can easily become a climber in a warmer one. Likewise, a lightly pruned shrub growing against a wall, even in a cooler climate, can easily be encouraged to climb up.

Most climbers have large flowers and stiff growth, are not too vigorous, and repeat-flower – although there are a number of exceptions. Climbing roses come, often as sports, from many different groups, including noisettes, hybrid teas, floribundas, ramblers, English roses, Bourbons, teas, Chinas, and hybrid perpetuals. So they are hugely variable, encompassing every size of flower, number of petals, type of fragrance, number of thorns, winter hardiness, and vigour. They are an immensely valuable group of plants, able to grow up and adorn a wide range of structures (see pp.170–203 for recommended varieties for various situations).

'Rambling Rector'

Ramblers

Ramblers generally have small flowers, lax growth, and do not repeat-flower. With their often extreme vigour, their main value is for growing up trees or over pergolas, where their flowers will hang down in festoons. The less vigorous varieties can also be grown against walls.

The early ramblers were simply crosses between climbing species like *Rosa wichurana*, *R. sempervirens*, *R. moschata*, *R. arvensis*, and *R. multiflora*, and various teas, hybrid perpetuals, and hybrid teas. This resulted in a wide range of different colours, flower sizes, and scents. *R. sempervirens* is more or less evergreen, and this has been passed on to some of its offspring, especially 'Félicité Perpétue' and the very beautiful 'Adélaïde d'Orléans' (p.200).

Modern breeding has succeeded in introducing repeat-flowering in a number of varieties (including 'The Lady of the Lake' and 'Gardens of Hex'). This usually means less vigour, and so a rambler that is easier to manage and place in the garden.

A number of ramblers, especially the bigger ones closest to the species like 'Francis E. Lester' (p.199), 'Rambling Rector' (p.150 and p.200), and *R. filipes* 'Kiftsgate' (p.199), set a superb crop of orange or red hips, some of which will last well into the winter.

ROSE
selector

Choosing the ideal rose

As roses can play a dominant role in a garden, often living 15–20 years or more, it is worth searching out varieties that are best-suited for their intended positions and conditions.

Look for roses with character, that will create the atmosphere you want – a wild thicket of single flowers followed by bright hips, perhaps; the romance and fragrance of old roses; or the exquisite formality of hybrid teas. What colours will work best? Pastel harmonies, or vivid contrasts?

Is repeat-flowering essential? Many roses can be in flower from early summer to late autumn. But once-flowering varieties are often full of character, and may be covered in hips through the autumn and winter – if they're not eaten by birds.

Where you want to plant the rose is also crucial: if the soil isn't as good as it might be, or it gets only a few hours of full sun each day, or is against a sun-baked wall, you'll need to select tough, disease-resistant varieties best-suited to those situations. It's also important to choose a rose of the right size – big enough to fill its spot, but not so big you're forever having to cut it back.

If you have the opportunity, seeing roses growing in a garden is always the best way to assess them. You want the whole plant to look good – individual flowers may look stunning in photographs but grow on an awkward-looking bush that will need some camouflage. Perhaps you'll find the colour isn't quite the shade you're after, or the fragrance is so seductive that you'll want to rethink your entire planting scheme to showcase it.

Sourcing roses

I have included a wide range of roses in this chapter. Some are commonly available in garden centres, others only from specialist nurseries in other countries. I wanted to include those I think are the very best for each category, and so a few roses appear multiple times: 'Gertrude Jekyll', for example, has a fabulous old rose perfume (p.146), but also makes an excellent short climber, really thriving on a sunny wall (p.172). Many entries include the original cultivar name the rose was first registered under, which may help when tracking it down, wherever you are in the world.

A rose-lover's garden
An assortment of varieties, including 'Mortimer Sackler' and 'Gertrude Jekyll', cover a pergola in this private London garden.

Roses for the front of a border

This is a great spot for smaller roses, especially ones with good fragrance. It's easy to fully appreciate a rose's beauty when it is planted at the front of the border. Shorter varieties won't get lost here, although some height variation will add interest.

'A Whiter Shade of Pale'

A Whiter Shade of Pale

HEIGHT *1m (3ft)* SPREAD *1m (3ft)*
FLOWERING *Repeat* TYPE *Hybrid tea*
SCENT *Medium sweet* CULTIVAR *'Peafanfare'*

If you're looking for a variety with the classically high-pointed centre of the hybrid tea flower, good health, and a tidy, upright habit, this rose is excellent. As the name suggests, it is a soft pink, making it easy to integrate into a colour scheme – sometimes a challenge with hybrid teas. Also good for growing in pots and for cutting.

Roald Dahl

HEIGHT *1m (3ft)* SPREAD *1m (3ft)*
FLOWERING *Repeat* TYPE *English rose*
SCENT *Medium tea* CULTIVAR *'Ausowlish'*

A lovely rounded shrub perfect for mixed borders, in a formal planting scheme, or as a hedge. The buds start a rich orange-red, then open into rounded soft-apricot flowers that are produced freely over a long period. With few thorns and excellent health, this is a delight.

'Roald Dahl'

'Empereur Charles IV'

'Scarborough Fair'

Scarborough Fair

HEIGHT *1m (3ft)* SPREAD *1m (3ft)* FLOWERING *Repeat*
TYPE *English rose* SCENT *Medium musky old rose*
CULTIVAR '*Ausoran*'

An unassuming but pretty rose that produces flowers from the ground up on a rounded shrub. The blush-pink flowers only have about 15 petals and are very open, showing off a central boss of bright yellow stamens. A particularly good choice at the front of a mixed border where its soft colouring will go well with any other flowers – even yellows. The fragrance is of medium strength, with old rose coming from the petals and musk from the stamens.

Empereur Charles IV

HEIGHT *75–100cm (2½–3ft)* SPREAD *75cm (2½ft)*
FLOWERING *Repeat* TYPE *Modern shrub* SCENT *Strong
myrrh and lily of the valley* CULTIVAR *'Vel15mscwi'*

A striking rose with strongly coloured and fragrant flowers.
The rounded, intensely fuchsia-pink blooms are medium-
sized and produced continuously on a healthy, neat, and
upright bush. With its strong perfume it is a wonderful
choice next to a path in front of taller roses or mixed in with
other plants. Also excellent as a cut flower.

Molineux

HEIGHT *100cm (3ft)* SPREAD *75cm (2½ft)* FLOWERING *Repeat*
TYPE *English rose* SCENT *Light to medium tea* CULTIVAR *'Ausmol'*

A neat and upright rose particularly good for more formal
plantings. The flowers, which form tight, many-petalled
rosettes, are produced freely and have a tea fragrance with a
musky background. While 'Molineux' is good planted en
masse, it also mixes well with other plants that soften its
upright shape, such as *Nepeta* (catmint); their colours also
complement each other beautifully.

Milhem Pemberton

HEIGHT *60–75cm (2–2½ft)* SPREAD *45cm (1½ft)*
FLOWERING *Repeat* TYPE *Modern shrub*
SCENT *Medium spice and herbs* CULTIVAR *'Vel14fecal'*

A rose that does everything! Its rich red flowers, paling to
carmine pink, are produced continuously from early summer
to late in the year, and if not dead-headed the later flowers
will produce a wonderful crop of large hips. Most varieties
of this size have no fragrance and are prone to disease, but
'Milhelm Pemberton' is excellent on both these counts.

'Molineux'

'Milhem Pemberton'

Sweet Haze

HEIGHT *60cm (2ft)* SPREAD *75cm (2½ft)*
FLOWERING *Repeat* TYPE *Floribunda*
SCENT *Slight* CULTIVAR *'Tan97274'*

This can be regarded either as a short, rounded shrub or a ground-cover rose, and is excellent as either. It is also good planted by a path – perhaps to grow partway across it – or in a mixed border. The single flowers are soft lilac-pink with long red stamens and are produced in large clusters, the petals dropping cleanly when each flower is finished. An award-winning, healthy plant.

Prins Alexander

HEIGHT *75cm (2½ft)* SPREAD *60cm (2ft)*
FLOWERING *Repeat* TYPE *Hybrid tea*
SCENT *Strong myrrh and ripe pears* CULTIVAR *'Vel17talma'*

A neat and tidy variety with blush-pink flowers, sometimes blended with apricot. At first, these have the high-pointed centre of a hybrid tea bloom, but they open up to form a neat bowl. They are strongly scented with a delicious blend of myrrh and ripe pears. A hardy rose with few thorns, this is a great choice to plant next to a path, in a container, or where space is limited.

Pearl Drift

HEIGHT *1m (3ft)* SPREAD *1.2m (4ft)*
FLOWERING *Repeat* TYPE *Modern shrub*
SCENT *Medium sweet* CULTIVAR *'Leggab'*

A particularly free-flowering, healthy rose. The buds start soft pink, opening to pretty, semi-double, pure white flowers with a sweet, musky fragrance. These are produced over a long period on a dense bush. 'Pearl Drift' is the product of two vigorous climbers, and while it is relatively short in temperate climates it can grow much taller in hot ones.

Lovely Parfuma

HEIGHT *75cm (2½ft)* SPREAD *60cm (2ft)*
FLOWERING *Repeat* TYPE *Floribunda*
SCENT *Very strong fruity* CULTIVAR *'Kortekcho'*

An award-winning, extremely healthy and highly fragrant rose, also known as 'Rosengrafin Marie Henriette'. The medium-pink flowers are very double, in the style of the old roses, and the fragrance changes from spicy and aniseed-like as the flower opens to fruity as it ages. 'Lovely Parfuma' forms a neat, upright shrub, making it a good choice for both formal and informal settings.

'Sweet Haze'

'Pearl Drift'

'Prins Alexander'

'Lovely Parfuma'

Roses for the middle of a border

Many rose varieties would suit the middle of a
border. I've focused on those around 1.2–1.5m (4–5ft)
tall, although of course you can adjust their height
by judicial pruning. They mix well with many
perennials of a similar height.

'Princess Alexandra of Kent'

Princess Alexandra of Kent

HEIGHT *1.2m (4ft)* SPREAD *1.2m (4ft)* FLOWERING *Repeat*
TYPE *English rose* SCENT *Strong tea* CULTIVAR *'Ausmerchant'*

A particularly beautiful variety with large, fragrant, very double blooms. The buds are pink with a hint of orange; when fully open the flowers are a warm, glowing pink, paling a little towards the outside. With about 130 petals in each, the flowers have a very strong fragrance that is initially tea but becomes more lemony with age. The plant is bushy and slightly arching – a lovely rounded shrub, excellent by a path or in a pot (p.118), where the fragrance can be easily appreciated. It mixes very well with other plants, especially those with blue flowers.

Lady of Shalott

HEIGHT *1.5m (5ft)* SPREAD *1.2m (4ft)*
FLOWERING *Repeat* TYPE *English rose*
SCENT *Medium to strong tea* CULTIVAR *'Ausnyson'*

An absolutely first-class variety that can be grown as a shrub or a climber. The flowers appear to be a rich apricot, although closer inspection shows that the insides of the petals are salmon-pink, whereas the outsides are more golden yellow. They are loosely double, meaning that the stamens are still accessible to bees. 'Lady of Shalott' flowers extremely freely, being hardly ever out of flower until late in the year. Tough and reliable, with slightly arching growth, it is best in a fairly large border, either with other roses or mixed in with perennials and shrubs.

Comte de Chambord

HEIGHT *1.2m (4ft)* SPREAD *1m (3ft)* FLOWERING *Repeat*
TYPE *Portland* SCENT *Strong old rose*

'Comte de Chambord' is a particularly lovely old rose, that has the advantage of repeat-flowering and fairly upright growth. The flowers are a pure rich pink, paling towards the outside. Its fragrance is one of the very best of any rose, so should be planted where it is easy to access. The growth is quite upright and it is not the healthiest of roses, but its other assets make up for this.

'Lady of Shalott'

'Comte de Chambord'

Thomas à Becket

HEIGHT *1.5m (5ft)*   SPREAD *1.2m (4ft)*
FLOWERING *Repeat*   TYPE *English rose*
SCENT *Medium old rose*   CULTIVAR *'Auswinston'*

'Thomas à Becket' is not too far removed from a species rose, which gives it a rather different character to the other English roses, and indeed to other roses generally. It is particularly valued for its medium-sized red flowers, which are shallowly cupped at first, the petals bending back as they open. It's quite an open shrub, flowering at the ends of long stems, making it well-suited for the middle or back of a border, to arch over shorter roses or other plants in front. The fragrance is old rose with a definite tinge of lemon zest.

Paula Vapelle

HEIGHT *1.5m (5ft)*   SPREAD *1.2m (4ft)*
FLOWERING *Repeat*   TYPE *Spinosissima hybrid*
SCENT *Medium fruity old rose*

The Scots rose (*R. spinosissima*) parentage gives this rose an interesting and most attractive appearance, something different to the norm. The pure white flowers are medium-sized and double with a central button eye, and are set off by the grey-green foliage. It has a delicious fragrance too, characteristic of this group of roses. It is very winter hardy.

'Paula Vapelle'

'Thomas à Becket'

'Caroline's Heart'

Caroline's Heart

HEIGHT *1.5m (5ft)*   SPREAD *1m (3ft)*
FLOWERING *Repeat*   TYPE *Modern shrub*
SCENT *Strong old rose*   CULTIVAR *'Vel16dsipo'*

An exceptionally free-flowering, versatile rose with a strong and delicious fragrance. The large, pure pink flowers appear full-petalled, although as they age the colour softens to pale pink, revealing the stamens. They are produced until late in the season, when a few hips appear alongside the flowers. The fragrance is mostly old rose but with hints of myrrh. 'Caroline's Heart' associates beautifully with perennials, biennials, or annuals in a mixed border, and is also well-suited to being grown in a pot or as a hedge. Very winter hardy.

Champagne Moment

HEIGHT *1.2m (4ft)* SPREAD *75cm (2½ft)*
FLOWERING *Repeat* TYPE *Floribunda*
SCENT *Light to medium* CULTIVAR *'Korvanaber'*

With softly coloured flowers and a neat, bushy habit, 'Champagne Moment' could be used in mixed borders or in more formal planting schemes. The blooms are soft apricot in the centre, paling to creamy white on the outside, and are produced in large clusters. The leaves are a dark, glossy green and particularly resistant to disease. Also known as 'Lions-Rose'.

Gabriel Oak

HEIGHT *1.2m (4ft)* SPREAD *1m (3ft)*
FLOWERING *Repeat* TYPE *English rose*
SCENT *Strong fruity* CULTIVAR *'Auscrowd'*

A valuable variety with strongly coloured, classically old rose flowers that stand out in the middle of a border. The blooms form a rosette and are a rich, deep pink. They are held on a vigorous, relatively upright shrub that would look lovely alongside shorter, softer pink flowers, be they roses or other plants. Lovely as a cut flower, especially with its strong fruity fragrance. A tough and reliable rose.

La Ville de Bruxelles

HEIGHT *1.5m (5ft)* SPREAD *1.2m (4ft)* FLOWERING *Once*
TYPE *Damask* SCENT *Strong fruity old rose*

A worthwhile variety, despite not repeat-flowering. The large flowers are classically old rose in character, the many pink petals arranged in a quartered effect with a button eye in the centre. They are set off by the large, healthy, pale-green leaves. 'La Ville de Bruxelles' takes a little time to mature and look its best, but it's worth the wait.

Vanessa Bell

HEIGHT *1.2m (4ft)* SPREAD *1m (3ft)*
FLOWERING *Repeat* TYPE *English rose*
SCENT *Medium to strong tea* CULTIVAR *'Auseasel'*

A lovely soft yellow variety, 'Vanessa Bell' is versatile, tough, and reliable. The young buds are tinged with pink, which soon disappears as they open into cup-shaped, full-petalled flowers, deeper yellow in the middle and creamy at the edge. It's a good idea to plant this variety close to a path so that the blooms can be easily accessed on a regular basis (they smell of green tea with touches of lemon and honey), and for ease of cutting to bring into the house. It is bushy but quite upright and so is an excellent choice for planting en masse, although it is equally good in small groups or even singly in a mixed border where the soft yellow works especially well with blues, purples, and lilacs.

'Champagne Moment'

'La Ville de Bruxelles'

'Gabriel Oak'

'Vanessa Bell'

Roses for
the back of
a border

Substantial roses that are 1.5m (5ft) or more
tall – and often the same across – are perfect
for a deep border that is backed by a wall,
fence, or hedge. They also look good as
specimens in a lawn, or as part of a shrubbery.

'Cornelia'

Cornelia

HEIGHT *1.5m (5ft)*   SPREAD *1.5m (5ft)*   FLOWERING *Repeat*
TYPE *Hybrid musk*   SCENT *Medium to strong tea*

With its gently arching growth, 'Cornelia' is ideal for the
back of a border, but will also look good as a single specimen
in a lawn. The individual flowers are quite small, about 5cm
(2in) across, a rich salmon-pink, and are produced very freely.
They look particularly beautiful and smell delicious in the
cooler weather of autumn. This is a healthy, vigorous rose and
in warmer climates it can easily become a sizeable climber.

Rosa californica 'Plena'

HEIGHT *2.5m (8ft)*   SPREAD *2m (6ft)*   FLOWERING *Once*
TYPE *Species rose*   SCENT *Strong old rose*

A worthwhile rose of very different character to modern
cultivars. It makes a large and magnificent shrub with great
quantities of relatively small, loosely double, mid-pink
flowers, and a delicious old rose fragrance. It will take a few
years to reach its full potential but is well worth the wait. It
also looks superb in a wild setting in long grass.

The Lark Ascending

HEIGHT *2m (6ft)*   SPREAD *2m (6ft)*   FLOWERING *Repeat*
TYPE *English rose*   SCENT *Light tea/myrrh*   CULTIVAR *'Ausursula'*

A really tough and reliable variety with rather upright
growth, 'The Lark Ascending' is ideal as a backdrop to blue
or purple perennials such as catmints, salvias, campanulas,
delphiniums, or asters. The flowers are loosely semi-double
and charming, and are produced freely from early summer
till late in the year. It is particularly healthy and winter hardy
too, surprisingly for a rose of this colour and height.

Rosa californica 'Plena'

'The Lark Ascending'

Hyde Hall

HEIGHT *2m (6ft)* SPREAD *2m (6ft)*
FLOWERING *Repeat* TYPE *English rose* SCENT *Light fruity*
CULTIVAR *'Ausbosky'*

This is an excellent choice for the back of a wide border. The fully double, mid-pink blooms are in the form of a shallow cup and make a great impression en masse – a wonderful backdrop for other roses or perennials. 'Hyde Hall' flowers freely, repeats well, and is very healthy.

Cinderella

HEIGHT *1.5m (5ft)* SPREAD *1m (3ft)*
FLOWERING *Repeat* TYPE *Modern shrub* SCENT *Strong fruity*
CULTIVAR *'Korfobalt'*

'Cinderella' has all the charm of the old roses, along with the advantages of the modern ones – good repeat-flowering and excellent health. The blooms are very double, with many petals beautifully arranged within an outer ring. The fragrance is strong and fruity – green apples with a hint of heliotrope. This rose is extremely healthy, and has won a number of gold medals in trials around Europe.

"With tall roses and other flowering shrubs, you can create a colourful, fragrance-filled shrubbery with year-round interest."

Thérèse Bugnet

HEIGHT *2m (6ft)* SPREAD *1.2m (4ft)*
FLOWERING *Repeat* TYPE *Rugosa hybrid* SCENT *Strong old rose*

This is a little-known rose with many excellent qualities. Looking at it, one might never guess that it is a hybrid of the super-thorny rugosa roses, since it is almost completely thornless — although its rather rough leaves do suggest such a parentage. The flowers are very much in the character of a full-petalled old rose and have the fragrance to match. 'Thérèse Bugnet' is extremely healthy and winter hardy, although happy in Mediterranean climates as well.

Westerland

HEIGHT *2m (6ft)* SPREAD *1.5m (5ft)*
FLOWERING *Repeat* TYPE *Modern shrub* SCENT *Strong fruity*
CULTIVAR *'Korwest'*

Some roses achieve fame quickly and others, like 'Westerland', take time. The flowers are large, over 10cm (4in) across, semi-double, and a real mix of vermillion, crimson, pink, yellow, and amber. While the unusual colour blend sometimes makes finding suitable partners difficult, the overall effect is not too harsh. The fragrance is strong and fruity, and it is very healthy. The flowers are followed by a good crop of long-lasting hips. Altogether an excellent variety.

Violacea

HEIGHT *2m (6ft)* SPREAD *1.5m (5ft)*
FLOWERING *Once* TYPE *Gallica*
SCENT *Light*

This is a splendid rose of real individuality, also known as 'La Belle Sultane'. Looking at it, one might imagine it is ancient and closely related to *Rosa gallica*, but in fact its origin is a mystery and it probably dates from the 19th century. The flowers are generally five-petalled and a rich magenta — almost black at the edges and white in the centre where there is a very fine boss of stamens. It makes a large shrub with long, almost thornless, arching stems.

'Penelope'

Penelope

HEIGHT *2m (6ft)*   SPREAD *2m (6ft)*   FLOWERING *Repeat*
TYPE *Hybrid musk*   SCENT *Medium to strong fruity musk*

'Penelope' makes an excellent backdrop and also a fine free-standing shrub, its arching stems covered in flowers from the ground up. These are semi-double, opening slightly blush-pink but quickly turning white. If dead-headed, it repeats well; if not, it will produce a heavy crop of distinctive coral-pink hips. The fragrance is an interesting mix of fruitiness from the petals and musk from the gold stamens. This is a rose that is tolerant of some shade and poorer soil. In Mediterranean climates it can easily become a climber.

Clair Matin

HEIGHT *2.5m (8ft); or 3m (10ft) as climber*
SPREAD *2m (6ft)*   FLOWERING *Repeat*
TYPE *Modern shrub*   SCENT *Light to medium sweet*
CULTIVAR *'Meimont'*

'Clair Matin' is outstanding for the freedom with which it flowers from early summer until the cold stops it. The young buds are a soft peach, opening out to pale pink semi-double flowers, making it a good backdrop for all colours. Given all the effort it puts into producing so many flowers, it responds well to generous feeding and good conditions, although it copes well without such help. Can also be grown as a climber.

'Clair Matin'

'Desdemona'

Roses for
mixed borders

These are roses of various heights that will look superb planted alongside other plants. Perennials, biennials, or annuals will set them off beautifully and offer the opportunity of introducing blue into your colour scheme. A mixture of plants also helps to keep roses healthy.

"Chief among its many advantages, the mixed border enhances the beauty of roses by juxtaposing them with other plants"

'Eustacia Vye'

Desdemona

HEIGHT *1m (3ft)* SPREAD *1m (3ft)*
FLOWERING *Repeat* TYPE *English rose*
SCENT *Strong fruity old rose* CULTIVAR *'Auskindling'*

Plants with pure white flowers can be difficult to integrate into a garden, sometimes looking a bit hard and clinical. The flowers of 'Desdemona', though, have a touch of blush in them, especially when young, and will combine beautifully with most other colours as long as they are not too strong. This is a free-flowering variety producing masses of chalice-shaped blooms. Though double, the flowers are not packed with petals and so get a lovely interplay of light and shadow within them. The fragrance is particularly delicious – a mix of old rose with hints of almond blossom, cucumber, and lemon zest, the latter sometimes coming very much to the fore. A rose that is also excellent in a container (p.123).

Eustacia Vye

HEIGHT *1.2m (4ft)* SPREAD *1m (3ft)* FLOWERING *Repeat*
TYPE *English rose* SCENT *Strong fruity* CULTIVAR *'Ausegdon'*

The soft pink and apricot colouring of 'Eustacia Vye' makes it an easy variety to incorporate in a mixed border. Its growth is quite upright, perfect behind something short such as *Erigeron karvinskianus*, *Nepeta*, or pinks (*Dianthus*), but make sure you can reach the flowers to smell their strong, fruity fragrance (p.142). It is a very healthy variety and repeat-flowers well.

Harlow Carr

HEIGHT *1m (3ft)* SPREAD *1m (3ft)* FLOWERING *Repeat*
TYPE *English rose* SCENT *Strong old rose* CULTIVAR *'Aushouse'*

Each flower of 'Harlow Carr' is a perfect medium-sized rosette of purest pink. They are produced freely in large clusters and have a strong old rose fragrance. The stems are quite arching, and flower from the ground up. 'Harlow Carr' is lovely as a cut flower, although beware its thorny stems! Also good in hedges (p.168).

'Harlow Carr'

'Felicia'

'Madame Hardy'

Madame Hardy

HEIGHT *1.5m (5ft); or 2.5m (8ft) as climber*
SPREAD *1.2m (4ft)* FLOWERING *Once*
TYPE *Damask* SCENT *Strong old rose*

One of the most beautiful of the old roses and one of the easiest to recognize. 'Madame Hardy' is one of the very few good white old roses, and its little green eye makes it an easy one to identify. The long green, leafy sepals are very characteristic too. The blooms are a perfectly formed rosette and deliciously fragrant. If lightly pruned it can get quite tall and even make a lovely climber.

Felicia

HEIGHT *1.5m (5ft); or 2.5m (8ft) as climber* SPREAD *1.5m (5ft)*
FLOWERING *Repeat* TYPE *Hybrid musk* SCENT *Medium to strong fruity musk*

One of the best hybrid musks, 'Felicia' flowers freely and is very healthy. The flowers are loosely double with petals that are rose-pink above and apricot below, giving an overall impression of a silvery salmon-pink. In the autumn the colour is richer and the flowers are produced in bigger clusters. If pruned lightly it can get quite big, and in warmer climates it can become a climber. Lovely mixed with other flowers.

Lichfield Angel

HEIGHT *1.2m (4ft)* SPREAD *1.2m (4ft)* FLOWERING *Repeat*
TYPE *English rose* SCENT *Light musk* CULTIVAR *'Ausrelate'*

A particularly free-flowering variety with rather lax, arching growth which looks superb with the many perennials of a similar habit. The flowers start a pale peachy pink, but when fully open are creamy white in the form of a loose rosette, the outer petals eventually reflexing back. Looks lovely with catmint in front of it and has the advantage of being practically thornless. Also makes a fine hedge.

The Lady Gardener

HEIGHT *1.2m (4ft)* SPREAD *1.2m (4ft)* FLOWERING *Repeat*
TYPE *English rose* SCENT *Strong tea* CULTIVAR *'Ausbrass'*

It is easy to find good bedfellows for roses with apricot flowers. The obvious ones are the purples of plants such as salvias, but by trying flowers of other colours you will soon find that many work well. With its strong, bushy growth, even one plant of 'The Lady Gardener' can make a statement (p.118), although a group of three planted closely together has an even better effect. It has a lovely fragrance, essentially tea with hints of cedarwood and vanilla.

'Lichfield Angel'

'The Lady Gardener'

Tuscany Superb

HEIGHT *1.5m (5ft)* SPREAD *1.2m (4ft)*
FLOWERING *Once* TYPE *Gallica*
SCENT *Light to medium old rose*

Roses with rich purple flowers always draw the eye and 'Tuscany Superb' is one of the best, despite only flowering once. The bunch of yellow stamens in the middle helps to emphasize the colour. Like nearly all gallicas it has very few prickles, and rubbing the young shoots releases a delicious, resinous smell. It looks particularly beautiful next to lavender.

Stéphanie d'Ursel

HEIGHT *1.2m (4ft)* SPREAD *1m (3ft)*
FLOWERING *Repeat* TYPE *Modern shrub* SCENT *Strong fruity*
CULTIVAR *'Vel15fchpo'*

A distinctive variety with large, almost single flowers of soft apricot that pale to cream, and so an easy rose to mix with stronger coloured flowers in the same colour range or a contrasting purple. The fragrance is unusual – lily of the valley with hints of lemon – so plant it where it is easily accessible, close to a path or in a container. Also attractive to bees and very healthy.

Belle de Jour

HEIGHT *1.2m (4ft)* SPREAD *1m (3ft)*
FLOWERING *Repeat*
TYPE *Floribunda*
SCENT *Strong vanilla and apricot*
CULTIVAR *'Deljaupar'*

'Belle de Jour' has very full flowers of lemon and creamy yellow with hints of salmon pink. They are produced on a neat and upright shrub. It is particularly healthy, and has won a number of awards in rose trials. The flowers are strongly fragrant – a lovely combination of vanilla and apricot. A good variety for cutting, too.

The Shepherdess

HEIGHT *1.2m (4ft)* SPREAD *1m (3ft)*
FLOWERING *Repeat*
TYPE *English rose* SCENT *Medium fruity* CULTIVAR *'Austwist'*

In any border it is important to have a balance of plants that demand attention and those that, while also beautiful and worthwhile, work well in the background. 'The Shepherdess' is a perfect example of such a variety. The blooms are a soft apricot, veering towards pink in some weathers, and the shape a deep cup with the stamens showing as the flower ages. It has a delicious fruity fragrance with hints of lemon.

Ipsilanté

HEIGHT *1.5m (5ft)* SPREAD *1.2m (4ft)*
FLOWERING *Once* TYPE *Gallica*
SCENT *Strong old rose*

A classic and very lovely gallica with fragrant, rich-pink flowers, which is also spelled 'Ypsilanté'. The arrangement of petals gives a roughly quartered effect, with a little green eye sometimes visible in the centre. The stems are quite lax and floppy, which means the flowers intermingle with those of their neighbours, creating beautiful colour combinations.

Nuits de Young

HEIGHT *1m (3ft)*
SPREAD *75cm (2½ft)*
FLOWERING *Once* TYPE *Moss*
SCENT *Strong old rose*

A distinctive rose and one of the darkest-flowered. It belongs to the moss group of roses that have varying amounts of soft mossy growth on their young stems and around the flowers. 'Nuits de Young' has plentiful quantities of this moss which, when rubbed, is sticky and smells deliciously of resin. The flowers have the classic old rose fragrance. It makes a slender, upright plant, so it is best to plant a few close together unless space is really tight. It looks superb next to strong pink flowers.

Princess Anne

HEIGHT *1.2m (4ft)* SPREAD *1.2m (4ft)*
FLOWERING *Repeat* TYPE *English rose*
SCENT *Medium tea* CULTIVAR *'Auskitchen'*

This is a variety that will stand out in a border with its big, bold flowers, the colour fading as it ages from a really rich, almost red-pink to mid-pink. It is a particularly tough and reliable rose that will cope well with less than ideal conditions and fit in perfectly with a wide range of other plants, as long as they are not planted so close that they compete with it for water and nutrients. It associates well with softer colours like the silver leaves of *Stachys byzantina* and *Artemisia* 'Powis Castle' as well as the lilac or lavender flowers of catmint, lavender, and salvia. The fragrance is variable, sometimes quite strong, other times not so.

Summer Memories

HEIGHT *1.2m (4ft)* SPREAD *60cm (2ft)*
FLOWERING *Repeat* TYPE *Modern shrub*
SCENT *Light* CULTIVAR *'Koruteli'*

A rose with the classic full-petalled flowers of the old roses. Good old roses with pure or creamy white flowers are difficult to find, so this is a useful alternative, especially as it has excellent disease resistance. An easy rose to mix into the middle of a border with shorter plants in front and (if space allows) taller ones behind.

'Summer Memories'

'Princess Anne' (mid-pink rose, right)

'Great Maiden's Blush'

Great Maiden's Blush

HEIGHT *2m (6ft)*   SPREAD *1.2m (4ft)*

FLOWERING *Once*   TYPE *Alba*   SCENT *Strong old rose*

This is one of the most beautiful of the old roses, and one of the oldest too, dating back to around 1550 or earlier. It has many other names, including 'Cuisse de Nymphe'. It is obviously a great survivor and will think nothing of competition from other plants or lack of care. The soft pink flowers, fading to white, are easy to integrate into a mixed border. Plant it where the blooms will be accessible so that their wonderful fragrance can be easily and regularly appreciated.

Tottering-by-Gently

HEIGHT *1.2m (4ft)* SPREAD *1.2m (4ft)*
FLOWERING *Repeat* TYPE *English rose*
SCENT *Light to medium musk* CULTIVAR *'Auscartoon'*

Roses with single flowers often look particularly effective in mixed borders, especially next to other single flowers such as cosmos and hollyhocks. 'Tottering-by-Gently' has medium-sized yellow blooms that if not dead-headed are followed by a superb crop of good-sized, long-lasting hips (p.159). The orange flowers of heleniums and geums would also be good company for this rose, as would any of the blue asters – *A.* x *frikartii* 'Mönch' and *Symphyotrichum* 'Little Carlow', for example.

Olivia Rose Austin

HEIGHT *1.2m (4ft)* SPREAD *1m (3ft)*
FLOWERING *Repeat* TYPE *English rose*
SCENT *Light to medium fruity* CULTIVAR *'Ausmixture'*

This is an outstanding rose both for the number of flowers it produces and its health. It starts flowering a good two to three weeks before most other roses and then repeats quickly and carries on till late in the year. The flowers open to shallow cups of mid-pink, set off nicely by the slightly grey tinge in the foliage. It can be used in many different ways in the garden, but it is perhaps best suited to mixing in with other plants. Different shades of pink will look lovely next to it, as will contrasting purples, blues, and even soft yellows.

Rosa gallica var. *officinalis*

HEIGHT *1.2m (4ft)* SPREAD *1m (3ft)*
FLOWERING *Once* TYPE *Gallica*
SCENT *Strong old rose*

Also known as the apothecary's rose, and the red rose of Lancaster, this may well be the oldest of the old roses to be found in gardens today. Grown in huge quantities in many parts of Europe, especially in the French town of Provins, it has long been used for culinary, medicinal, and cosmetic purposes. The flowers are quite large, magenta-pink and semi-double, with contrasting yellow stamens. It is particularly tough and will not be too troubled by competition from invading perennials. Hips follow the flowers, although they are a rather dull red.

For Your Eyes Only

HEIGHT *1m (3ft)* SPREAD *75cm (2½ft)*
FLOWERING *Repeat* TYPE *Floribunda*
SCENT *Light, lemon* CULTIVAR *'Cheweyesup'*

With its single, salmon-pink flowers and plum-red central eye, this rose is the result of attempts by breeders to introduce the distinct red eye of the species rose *Rosa persica* into modern, repeat-flowering varieties. For Your Eyes Only is healthy and free-flowering, but its most notable feature is that central eye: picking out this darker shade for neighbouring plants would work well.

'Tottering-by-Gently'

Rosa gallica var. *officinalis*

'Olivia Rose Austin'

'For Your Eyes Only'

Roses for containers

A rose in a container is a wonderful way of bringing colour and perfume to a patio, deck, balcony, or any area where it is not possible to plant anything in the ground. The best varieties are small, rounded, and have a delicious fragrance.

The Lady Gardener

HEIGHT *1.2m (4ft)* SPREAD *1.2m (4ft)*
FLOWERING *Repeat* TYPE *English rose*
SCENT *Strong tea* CULTIVAR *'Ausbrass'*

With its rather upright, bushy growth, 'The Lady Gardener' is a substantial and beautiful rose for a pot. The large apricot flowers have the most delicious tea fragrance with hints of cedarwood and vanilla. Placing the container against a light-coloured wall would help to set the flowers off and encourage earlier flowering. A healthy rose that will repeat-flower well.

Princess Alexandra of Kent

HEIGHT *1.2m (4ft)* SPREAD *1.2m (4ft)*
FLOWERING *Repeat* TYPE *English rose*
SCENT *Strong tea and fruit* CULTIVAR *'Ausmerchant'*

The large rich-pink flowers of 'Princess Alexandra of Kent' make a statement in a pot. Its strong tea fragrance with a lemon finish, its toughness, and its reliability are also ideal characteristics for a container-grown rose. In the border (p.97) it is a fairly upright, bushy plant, but in a pot, with more light around the base, it becomes more rounded and produces flowers lower down.

'The Lady Gardener'

'Princess Alexandra of Kent'

Herzogin Christiana

HEIGHT *75cm (2½ft)*
SPREAD *45cm (1½ft)*
FLOWERING *Repeat*
TYPE *Floribunda*
SCENT *Strong fruit*
CULTIVAR *'Korgeowim'*

This is a neat, fairly upright variety, with soft-pink flowers that would look pretty in a blue glazed pot. The blooms are a little unusual, being very rounded and only opening up partially. They are soft-pink in the middle and more of a creamy white on the outer petals. The fruity fragrance is particularly strong – a lovely mix of lemon, raspberries, and apple.

Natasha Richardson

HEIGHT *1m (3ft)*
SPREAD *75cm (2½ft)*
FLOWERING *Repeat*
TYPE *Floribunda*
SCENT *Strong citrus*
CULTIVAR *'Harpacket'*

An attractive, compact rose with flowers very much in the style of the old roses. As the flowers age, they open up to reveal the stamens. 'Natasha Richardson' has a delightful citrus fragrance, refreshing if you place the pot by a seating area. It is extremely healthy and repeat-flowers well.

Sibelius

HEIGHT *1m (3ft)*
SPREAD *75cm (2½ft)*
FLOWERING *Repeat*
TYPE *Hybrid musk*
SCENT *Medium*
CULTIVAR *'Lenbar'*

'Sibelius' produces an abundance of small, semi-double flowers that vary in colour between light purple and deep pink, very reminiscent of the once-flowering rambler 'Veilchenblau'. This small shrub rose flowers repeatedly throughout the summer and into the autumn when, if not dead-headed, red hips are formed. At the same time, the leaves change colour from dark green to shades of red and yellow. A rather different, pretty rose.

Joie de Vivre

HEIGHT *60cm (2ft)*
SPREAD *45cm (1½ft)*
FLOWERING *Repeat*
TYPE *Floribunda*
SCENT *Light*
CULTIVAR *'Korfloci01'*

A compact and extremely healthy variety perfect for a smaller pot in a more confined area. The pretty blooms are in the style of an old rose, with many petals arranged in a rosette, the colour being a soft apricot-pink, paling towards the outside. An award-winning, extremely healthy rose, also known as 'Garden of Roses'.

Gartenprinzessin Marie-José

HEIGHT *75cm (2½ft)*
SPREAD *60cm (2ft)*
FLOWERING *Repeat*
TYPE *Floribunda*
SCENT *Strong fruit*
CULTIVAR *'Korgehaque'*

An excellent rose, perfect for a container. The deep pink flowers initially form balls which eventually open up to reveal the centre. The fragrance is particularly strong, essentially fruity with distinct notes of raspberry and rhubarb and a hint of patchouli. A naturally compact variety, 'Gartenprinzessin Marie-José' won't need a huge pot or take up too much space. It is extremely healthy and winter hardy.

"A pot-grown rose becomes a focal point – especially so if it's a small variety that might otherwise get lost in a mixed bed."

'Golden Beauty'

'Desdemona'

Golden Beauty

HEIGHT *1m (3ft)*   SPREAD *1m (3ft)*   FLOWERING *Repeat*
TYPE *Floribunda*   SCENT *Medium sweet*   CULTIVAR *'Korberbeni'*

As its name suggests, this rose has rich golden-yellow flowers set off by dark-green leaves. At the bud stage the flowers have the classic high-pointed centre of a hybrid tea, but then open up to reveal gold stamens. 'Golden Beauty' is extremely healthy (it is a winner of many awards) and flourishes in the hot conditions often found on a patio, terrace, or balcony.

Desdemona

HEIGHT *1m (3ft)*   SPREAD *1m (3ft)*   FLOWERING *Repeat*
TYPE *English rose*   SCENT *Strong fruity old rose*
CULTIVAR *'Auskindling'*

With its strong, delicious fragrance and excellent freedom of flowering, 'Desdemona' is a good choice for containers. It is not too tall or vigorous and will be happy in a medium-sized pot although, as with all roses in containers, it is important to keep it well watered to encourage maximum flowering. The soft creamy white flowers look good in a blue pot.

Marie Pavié

HEIGHT *60cm (2ft)*   SPREAD *75cm (2½ft)*   FLOWERING *Repeat*
TYPE *Polyantha*   SCENT *Strong musk*

'Marie Pavié' (also spelled 'Pavič') was introduced towards the end of the 19th century and remains a good rose, especially in containers. The scent is musky, the type that floats on the air, and so can be enjoyed even if sitting some distance away. The soft-pink flowers, fading to white, are produced almost ceaselessly from summer to autumn.

'Marie Pavié'

Roses for
tight spaces

These roses are all short in stature or narrow in width, to
fit into small gardens and odd gaps. The flowers are small
or medium-sized, and variable in petal count and form, ranging
from single to very double – just like an old rose. These are
also good choices for smaller containers.

'Sweet Honey'

Sweet Honey

HEIGHT *100cm (3ft)* SPREAD *75cm (2½ft)*
FLOWERING *Repeat* TYPE *Floribunda*
SCENT *Light* CULTIVAR *'Kormecaso'*

As the name suggests, 'Sweet Honey' has beautifully formed soft-apricot flowers that gradually open up to reveal gold stamens and then pale to creamy white with age, giving a lovely mixed effect. It is very healthy and perfect for small borders or as a hedge.

Absolutely Fabulous

HEIGHT *100cm (3ft)* SPREAD *60cm (2ft)* FLOWERING *Repeat*
TYPE *Floribunda* SCENT *Medium to strong myrrh*
CULTIVAR *'Wekvossutono'*

Since its introduction in 2004, this has become a firm favourite in many parts of the world, a reflection not only of its qualities but its ability to flourish in different climates. The flowers are a warm golden-yellow, paling with age to creamy white. It has a good myrrh fragrance, although some perceive it as more like aniseed. It is particularly free-flowering and healthy. An excellent choice for a small border, on its own or planted as a group of two or three or more if space allows. Also good in more formal bedding areas.

Dolomiti

HEIGHT *75cm (2½ft)* SPREAD *45cm (1½ft)*
FLOWERING *Repeat* TYPE *Floribunda*
SCENT *Light* CULTIVAR *'Korrahibe'*

'Dolomiti' (also known as 'Olijdolo') is a particularly free-flowering and healthy variety that will cheer up a border or container for many months. It is tough and reliable, and has won many awards around Europe. The wide-open, almost single flowers are a bright pink on the outside with a contrasting white centre. With the advent of the cooler weather hips can be allowed to form, providing colour for several more months.

'Absolutely Fabulous'

'Dolomiti'

Lupo

HEIGHT *45cm (1½ft)*   SPREAD *30cm (1ft)*
FLOWERING *Repeat*   TYPE *Miniature*
SCENT *Light*   CULTIVAR *'Kordwarul'*

A lovely little rose that is suitable for pots and can also be bought as a standard. The small semi-double flowers are dark purple to carmine red, produced in great profusion, and well-loved by bees. 'Lupo' copes well with both heat and shade, so is particularly good for balconies, raised beds, and the edge of a path or border. If not dead-headed it will produce a profusion of hips. It has excellent disease resistance.

Summer of Love

HEIGHT *75cm (2½ft)*   SPREAD *45cm (1½ft)*
FLOWERING *Repeat*   TYPE *Floribunda*
SCENT *Light*   CULTIVAR *'Korfliaumi'*

A brightly coloured rose with flowers that are yellow in the centre and cherry red at the edges. A good variety to create some excitement in a border, perhaps next to more subdued roses, perennials, or annuals. Bees love the flowers and help to ensure a good crop of hips in the autumn. An award-winning plant, it is extremely resistant to disease.

Wildfire

HEIGHT *60cm (2ft)*   SPREAD *45cm (1½ft)*
FLOWERING *Repeat*   TYPE *Patio*
SCENT *Light*   CULTIVAR *'Fryessex'*

A brightly coloured, compact little rose that will brighten up any corner. The loosely double flowers are glowing orange and are produced freely over a long season. It would also make a good choice for a container or a raised bed and can be bought as a standard.

Miss Edith Cavell

HEIGHT *60cm (2ft)*   SPREAD *45cm (1½ft)*
FLOWERING *Repeat*   TYPE *Dwarf polyantha*
SCENT *Light*

This is a sport (one of many) from the 'Orléans Rose' that plays such an important part in the history of rose breeding, appearing in the ancestry of nearly every subsequent polyantha and floribunda. The 'Orléans Rose' has small semi-double or double cherry-red flowers, whereas 'Miss Edith' is slightly darker and is particularly free-flowering and healthy. Interestingly, the flower stalks have glandular hairs that smell resinous, like the gallicas.

'Lupo'

'Wildfire'

'Summer of Love'

'Miss Edith Cavell'

'Sternenhimmel'

'Pink Hit'

'Katharina Zeimet' (white blooms, beneath birch trees) as part of a mixed border display

Sternenhimmel

HEIGHT *30cm (1ft)*   SPREAD *30cm (1ft)*
FLOWERING *Repeat*   TYPE *Miniature*
SCENT *Light*   CULTIVAR *'Korhubkah'*

A very small rose suitable for very small spaces. The flowers are only 4cm (1½in) across and loved by bees. They are single or with just the odd extra petal or two and are soft-pink, paling slightly with age. 'Sternenhimmel' repeat-flowers well but is willing, given the chance, to produce quantities of hips. A particularly healthy variety.

Pink Hit

HEIGHT *30cm (1ft)*   SPREAD *30cm (1ft)*
FLOWERING *Repeat*   TYPE *Miniature*
SCENT *None*   CULTIVAR *'Poultipe'*

It is worth looking closely at the flowers of miniature roses. Some, like 'Pink Hit' (also known as 'Silver Wishes'), have the most perfect, fully double, old rose style blooms. The colour too would be exactly right – a pure pink. Unlike the true old roses, though, this is an excellent repeater that lacks scent. It is tough, reliable, grows and flowers well in poorer soils, and is also ideal for a container.

Katharina Zeimet

HEIGHT *100cm (3ft)*   SPREAD *75cm (2½ft)*
FLOWERING *Repeat*   TYPE *Dwarf polyantha*
SCENT *Medium sweet*

This is one of the longest-flowering roses. While the individual white flowers are not particularly shapely, they bloom in huge quantities, with large fragrant clusters appearing throughout a long flowering period. If lightly pruned, or grown in warm climates, 'Katharina Zeimet' can get substantially taller. Very winter hardy.

'Comte de Champagne'

Roses for wildlife

Roses of all sizes and types can be excellent for encouraging wildlife into your garden. The varieties showcased here all have single or semi-double flowers, to encourage as many beneficial insects into the garden as possible. Many also produce hips, a valuable food source during the winter months, while their stems offer cover for birds and small mammals.

'Weg der Sinne'

Comte de Champagne

HEIGHT *1.2m (4ft)*   SPREAD *1.2m (4ft)*
FLOWERING *Repeat*   TYPE *English rose*
SCENT *Light to medium musk*   CULTIVAR *'Ausufo'*

'Comte de Champagne' has simple but charming semi-double flowers which, with their large number of stamens, are most attractive to bees. The apricot young flowers and soft creamy-yellow older ones make for a lovely mix of different shades, making it an easy rose to incorporate into a border.

Weg der Sinne

HEIGHT *75cm (2½ft)*   SPREAD *60cm (2ft)*
FLOWERING *Repeat*   TYPE *Modern shrub*
SCENT *Light*   CULTIVAR *'Korwedesi'*

A tough, shade-tolerant and versatile rose well-suited to edges of borders, as well as containers for the terrace or balcony. The flowers are a strong violet-purple with a contrasting yellow ring in the middle from both the stamens and the base of the petals. A good crop of hips forms later in the year. Very winter hardy.

Dunwich Rose

HEIGHT *60cm (2ft)*   SPREAD *1m (3ft)*
FLOWERING *Once*   TYPE *Species rose*   SCENT *Light*

This is a form of *Rosa spinosissima*, which is found around the coasts of the British Isles and Europe growing on sand dunes. 'Dunwich Rose' is different in having lovely arching stems which are covered in creamy white flowers early in the season. It does not produce the black hips or have the delicious fragrance of the original species, but it does have the advantage of not spreading quite so vigorously. Very thorny and extremely tough.

'Dunwich Rose'

Morning Mist

HEIGHT *2m (6ft)*   SPREAD *1.5m (5ft)*
FLOWERING *Repeat*   TYPE *English rose*
SCENT *Light musk*   CULTIVAR *'Ausfire'*

A large and eye-catching rose for the back of the border or a wilder area. The flowers are single, and are a strong shade of coral pink with a large boss of stamens with red filaments. While the colour might sound a little tricky it is in fact not too bright and not difficult to find good partners for. The flowers are followed by large orange hips that last right through the winter.

Rosa × richardii

HEIGHT *1m (3ft)*   SPREAD *1.2m (4ft)*
FLOWERING *Single*   TYPE *Species hybrid*
SCENT *Light musk*

The origin of this rose (also known as *R. sancta*) is a real mystery. Stems with identical blooms were found in Egyptian tombs dating as far back as 200 CE, but there is no certain history of it in cultivation before 1890. Whatever its history it is a beautiful rose, with large single species-like flowers that start soft pink, paling to blush. The petals are slightly crumpled, not unlike those of the rock rose (*Cistus*). It may be a cross between *R. gallica* and *R. arvensis*, the first supplying its large flowers and the second its elegant arching growth. Unfortunately it produces hardly any hips, but it is attractive to insects. It is tough, growing well even in difficult positions.

Polyantha Grandiflora

HEIGHT *7m (23ft)*   SPREAD *5m (16ft)*
FLOWERING *Once*   TYPE *Rambler*
SCENT *Strong musk*

This is one of the best roses for bees – when it's in flower the buzzing can be heard from some distance away. The individual blooms are a little larger than those of most wild roses and slightly on the creamy side of white. They have a strong and delicious musky fragrance which can be smelled almost before the rose is seen. At close quarters it is more clove-like. Great quantities of small red hips are produced which will last through the winter unless taken by the birds. The leaves too are attractive – glossy and with a crimson midrib. An excellent choice for growing up a tree or somewhere where it can be allowed to spread at will. Also excellent for arrangements, whether in summer with the flowers or winter with the hips.

Topolina

HEIGHT *45cm (1½ft)*   SPREAD *60cm (2ft)*
FLOWERING *Repeat*   TYPE *Modern shrub*
SCENT *Light*   CULTIVAR *'Korpifleu'*

The great mass of stamens in the middle of each flower of 'Topolina' is hugely attractive to bees and other insects. The blooms, which are produced very freely, are single and a fairly bright pink with a soft yellow eye. The rose is award-winning and extremely healthy. A good choice for the edge of a path or as ground cover.

'Morning Mist'

'Polyantha Grandiflora'

Rosa x richardii

'Topolina'

"While roses lack nectar, their pollen is highly nutritious, providing a valuable food source to bees, hoverflies, beetles, and other insects."

Bee's Paradise White

HEIGHT *60cm (2ft)*   SPREAD *45cm (1½ft)*
FLOWERING *Repeat*   TYPE *Modern shrub*
SCENT *None*

'Bee's Paradise White' (also known as 'Bienenwiede Weiss') produces an abundance of white semi-double flowers that are extremely attractive to bees. It forms a relaxed-looking shrub that is sturdy and disease-resistant. It is a good choice for the front of a border, a raised bed, or a container, and mixes well with pastel-coloured plants.

'Bee's Paradise White'

'Fortuna' (shown in foreground with *Hosta* 'Cripula')

'The Lady's Blush'

Fortuna

HEIGHT *60cm (2ft)*   SPREAD *45cm (1½ft)*
FLOWERING *Repeat*   TYPE *Modern shrub*
SCENT *Light*   CULTIVAR *'Koratomi'*

A pretty, softly coloured variety with masses of flowers that are particularly attractive to pollinators. The salmon-pink flowers pale to blush, giving a lovely mix of colours. It has a fairly bushy, upright habit that is easy to mix in with other plants, especially those with blue, lilac, or purple flowers. Very healthy.

The Lady's Blush

HEIGHT *1.2m (4ft)*   SPREAD *1m (3ft)*
FLOWERING *Repeat*   TYPE *English rose*
SCENT *Light*   CULTIVAR *'Ausoscar'*

A medium-sized shrub, 'The Lady's Blush' produces great quantities of semi-double flowers that are loved by bees. They are a soft mid-pink with a white eye and a central ring of red where the stamens are attached. If not dead-headed, hips will follow the flowers. A tough and reliable rose for the middle of a border or in a wilder area.

Roses for wild areas

The species roses and their near relatives are perfect for wilder parts of the garden, fitting especially well into meadow and prairie-style planting. They have beautiful flowers and hips, and sometimes autumn leaf colour too. Some are quite compact, while others – given the chance – will scramble up into trees. Most are tolerant of poorer soils.

Rosa hugonis

Rosa hugonis

HEIGHT *2.5m (8ft)*   SPREAD *2m (6ft)*
FLOWERING *Once*   TYPE *Species rose*   SCENT *Light*

This is perhaps the most beautiful of all the yellow wild roses, and indeed of all the species. The flowers are a soft primrose-yellow with a bunch of golden yellow stamens in the centre which bees are very attracted to. The foliage is tiny and fern-like. *Rosa hugonis* will take a few years to reach maturity, during which time it shouldn't be pruned, so it is important to make sure it has the space to reach its full potential.

Rosa canina

HEIGHT *3m (10ft)*   SPREAD *2.5m (8ft)*
FLOWERING *Once*   TYPE *Species rose*   SCENT *Light*

This is the familiar dog rose, native to the British Isles and much of Europe, with simple five-petalled flowers that somehow are so beautiful. Their colour is usually a soft rose pink but varies from deep pink to almost white. It is a vigorous rose that can easily scramble high up into a tree, so its positioning needs to be carefully considered. It will still flower freely even if planted in a hedge and trimmed regularly. The flowers are followed by long, oval, vermillion hips. There are a few hybrids of *Rosa canina*, the outstanding one being *R. × hibernica*, which produces a fine crop of extremely long-lasting dark-red hips.

Rosa canina

Complicata

HEIGHT *1.5m (5ft); or 3m (10ft) as climber*
SPREAD *2m (6ft)* FLOWERING *Once*
TYPE *Species hybrid* SCENT *Light*

This is not a true species rose but a hybrid between *Rosa gallica* and *R. canina*. The large flowers (13cm/5in across) are rose-pink with a white centre and have a large clump of stamens. As a shrub it has quite vigorous and rather lax growth, which encourages a profusion of flowers. It also makes an attractive climber. The flowers are followed by large red hips. It looks beautiful planted among long grass and oxeye daisies.

Rosa virginiana

HEIGHT *1.5m (5ft)* SPREAD *1.2m (4ft)*
FLOWERING *Once* TYPE *Species rose* SCENT *Light*

Unlike many species roses, *Rosa virginiana* doesn't grow too big and so works well in medium-sized gardens. The cerise-pink flowers start to appear quite late, after midsummer, but continue for a good six weeks. By October the shiny round hips colour up to a bright red, and can stay on until the following spring. The leaves too are attractive, being quite brightly coloured in spring and then again later in the year when a whole range of glorious autumnal tints appears. The stems are red-brown in winter and relatively thornless. In addition, this rose is extremely tough and will grow well in both shade and poor soil.

Rosa spinosissima 'Single Cherry'

HEIGHT *1.2m (4ft)* SPREAD *1m (3ft)*
FLOWERING *Once* TYPE *Spinosissima hybrid*
SCENT *Strong old rose*

An immediately recognizable rose, each of the petals being a vivid cherry red on the upper side and silvery blush on the reverse. The rich golden-yellow stamens stand out against the dark background, adding to the beauty of the flower. Out of flower it is obviously a spinosissima hybrid, with small dark-green leaves and thorny stems. Like the others of this group it will grow well (and sucker freely) even in poor, sandy soil.

Rosa nutkana

HEIGHT *2m (6ft)* SPREAD *1.2m (4ft)*
FLOWERING *Once* TYPE *Species rose* SCENT *Light*

While most wild roses will grow into very large shrubs, *Rosa nutkana* is rather smaller and so easier to fit in. The flowers are lilac-pink, slightly darker in the middle, which creates an effective background for the golden yellow stamens. The round orange-red hips are very persistent. An easy and trouble-free rose to grow.

'Complicata'

Rosa spinosissima 'Single Cherry'

Rosa virginiana

Rosa nutkana

Rosa xanthina 'Canary Bird'

Rosa palustris

Rosa palustris

HEIGHT *1.2m (4ft)* SPREAD *1.2m (4ft)*
FLOWERING *Once* TYPE *Species rose*
SCENT *Light to medium*

In its native North America, *Rosa palustris* goes by the common name "swamp rose", although it grows just as happily, if not better, in poor, sandy soils. The flowers start quite late, continuing well into late summer, and are a pure mid-pink. They are larger than those of most species roses, especially the North American ones. *Rosa palustris* does produce hips, although they are not particularly large or noticeable. It's a perfect rose for a wild area, where it will sucker quite freely.

Rosa xanthina 'Canary Bird'

HEIGHT *2.5m (8ft)* SPREAD *2.2m (7ft)* FLOWERING *Once*
TYPE *Species rose* SCENT *Light*

As the name suggests, the flowers (which bees love) are a bright yellow, borne freely on long, arching stems, and making a bold statement in mid- to late spring. The foliage is attractive too, the leaflets being small and almost fern-like. The hips are round and maroon. 'Canary Bird' can be subject to dieback, although less so on well-drained soils or in drier climates. Planting deeply encourages it to produce more roots, lessening this risk.

Rosa sweginzowii

HEIGHT *3m (10ft)* SPREAD *3m (10ft)* FLOWERING *Once*
TYPE *Species rose* SCENT *Light*

Rosa sweginzowii makes a large and very thorny shrub that in summer is covered in flowers. The flowers are mid-pink, with just the very centre below the creamy yellow stamens being white. They are followed by long, shiny orange-red hips, the long sepals remaining attached. These sepals have aromatic hairs which, when rubbed, give off the same resinous smell as the moss roses. A rose much loved by bees.

Rosa primula

HEIGHT *2m (6ft)* SPREAD *2.5m (8ft)*
FLOWERING *Once* TYPE *Species rose*
SCENT *Light, but the leaves smell strongly*

This is one of the few roses whose leaves have a distinct smell. On humid evenings, or if crushed, they smell strongly of incense. They are attractive in their own right, with as many as 15 slender leaflets on each stem. *Rosa primula* starts flowering early in the year, the flowers being a pale primrose-yellow. They are followed by round red hips, although these aren't showy. Like the other species roses, it should be allowed to grow without any pruning.

Rosa sweginzowii

Rosa primula

'Boscobel'

Roses for scent

Perfume is an essential aspect of the mystique and character of many roses, and it comes in a surprising variety of aromas – not just the classic old rose, but all kinds of fruity and spicy notes. While countless roses are scented, these outstandingly fragrant varieties are roses to plant beside your favourite seat in the garden, to enjoy as you relax.

Eustacia Vye

HEIGHT *1.2m (4ft)* SPREAD *1m (3ft)*
FLOWERING *Repeat* TYPE *English rose*
SCENT *Strong fruity* CULTIVAR *'Ausegdon'*

An excellent variety with beautiful blooms that have a strong and deliciously fruity fragrance. The flowers start as deep cups gradually opening up to reveal the many petals, which have a slightly ruffled look to them. They are a soft glowing apricot-pink, paling with age, and are held on fairly upright stems. An excellent choice for a more formal bed, a mixed border, or as a hedge, even in some shade.

'Eustacia Vye'

Boscobel

HEIGHT *1m (3ft)* SPREAD *1m (3ft)* FLOWERING *Repeat*
TYPE *English rose* SCENT *Strong myrrh* CULTIVAR *'Auscousin'*

One of the strongest and most distinctive fragrances to be
found in the English roses – essentially myrrh with additional
hints of hawthorn, elderflower, pear, and almond. The
flowers are cup-shaped, filled with many petals varying in
colour from pink through to apricot. A healthy and fairly
upright shrub with upward-pointing blooms, perfect for the
mixed border.

Paul's Himalayan Musk

HEIGHT *12m (40ft)* SPREAD *5m (16ft)* FLOWERING *Once*
TYPE *Rambler* SCENT *Strong musk*

Although not quite in the top league for vigour, this rose
certainly is for its strong musk fragrance, which wafts from it
for some distance. This comes from the vast numbers of
small semi-double soft-pink flowers. As it is such a big rose,
it should only be grown into a big tree, otherwise it will be a
real challenge to keep under control. It may take a few years
to create a good show, but it is well worth the wait if you
have the space.

Buttercup

HEIGHT *1.5m (5ft)* SPREAD *1.2m (4ft)* FLOWERING *Repeat*
TYPE *English rose* SCENT *Strong* CULTIVAR *'Ausband'*

For many years the fragrances of the roses at David Austin
Roses were identified by Robert Calkin. He was an expert at
describing them, naming each element. The exception was
'Buttercup', for which he could only offer 'strong and
delicious'. It is sometimes reminiscent of orange blossom and
just occasionally cocoa powder! The flowers are semi-double,
a pure golden-yellow, and held in large, open sprays. It can
get quite tall, so is best towards the back of a mixed border,
but make sure it is still accessible.

'Paul's Himalayan Musk'

'Buttercup'

Rose de Rescht

HEIGHT *1m (3ft)*
SPREAD *75cm (2½ft)*
FLOWERING *Repeat*
TYPE *Portland* SCENT *Strong old rose*

An excellent Portland (also known as 'De Resht'), rather shorter and neater than 'Jacques Cartier' but with the same strong and delicious old rose fragrance. The flowers are very neat, medium-sized, and of a colour that is difficult to describe, especially as it can vary with the weather. A pale crimson or bright magenta would be the closest. A tough and healthy rose, with fresh green leaves. It looks good mixed with perennials or even as a short hedge.

Jacques Cartier

HEIGHT *1.2m (4ft)*
SPREAD *1m (3ft)*
FLOWERING *Repeat*
TYPE *Portland* SCENT *Strong old rose*

Also known as 'Marchesa Boccella', this variety is arguably the best of the Portlands. The fragrance is strong, pure old rose and the flowers epitomize an old rose, with their mass of petals beautifully arranged around a central eye. The growth is upright, so it's best grown with other plants around it. It will cope well with quite significant shade. An excellent all-rounder.

Graham Thomas

HEIGHT *1.2m (4ft); or 3m (10ft)
as climber* SPREAD *1.2m (4ft)*
FLOWERING *Repeat*
TYPE *English rose*
SCENT *Medium to strong tea*
CULTIVAR *'Ausmas'*

Tea fragrance can sometimes be hard to recognize, but in 'Graham Thomas' it is obvious and particularly delicious, with a lovely cool violet character. This rose can be grown as a reasonably tall shrub or, in a warm location, makes an excellent climber (p.193). The flowers are cup-shaped and an extraordinarily rich shade of yellow.

Munstead Wood

HEIGHT *1.2m (4ft)*
SPREAD *1m (3ft)*
FLOWERING *Repeat*
TYPE *English rose*
SCENT *Fruity old rose*
CULTIVAR *'Ausbernard'*

A richly coloured rose with a rich fragrance – a perfect mix of old rose and fruit (more specifically blackberry, blueberry, and damson). The blooms are large, full-petalled, and a deep, velvety crimson, a little paler on the undersides of the petals. It will make a real impact in a border, especially when planted next to blue flowers. Responds to a little extra care and attention. Very thorny!

Sophie's Perpetual

HEIGHT *1.5m (5ft)*
SPREAD *1.2m (4ft)*
FLOWERING *Repeat*
TYPE *China* SCENT *Strong*

Robert Calkin described the scent of 'Sophie's Perpetual' as the closest to a real perfume, and it is indeed delicious. The flowers are medium-sized, a soft pink which darkens with age – normal for the Chinas but unusual for most other roses – to a light crimson. It takes some time to build up to a substantial shrub and so is best pruned lightly. A pretty and rather unusual rose.

Céline Forestier

HEIGHT *2m (6ft); or 4m (13ft) as a climber* SPREAD *2m (6ft)*
FLOWERING *Repeat* TYPE *Noisette*
SCENT *Strong tea*

A very lovely rose best suited to warmer climates, but worth trying in the UK if given a warm, protected wall to grow up. It has a really delicious, rich, pure tea fragrance. The buds are dark pink, opening up to a soft yellow that pales to cream at the outside. The petals have a silky texture. 'Céline Forestier' can be grown as a large shrub (which is a good way of encouraging lots of flowers), as well as a climber.

'Ispahan'

'Constance Spry'

Ispahan

HEIGHT *1.5m (5ft)* SPREAD *1.2m (4ft)*

FLOWERING *Once* TYPE *Damask* SCENT *Strong old rose*

One of the very best of the old roses, 'Ispahan' has beautiful blooms and a strong and delicious old rose fragrance. The flowers are pure mid-pink and open to perfectly formed rosettes. It is the first of the damasks to start flowering and the last to stop, and also has the advantage of being semi-evergreen.

Constance Spry

HEIGHT *2m (6ft); or 3m (10ft) as a climber* SPREAD *2m (6ft)*

FLOWERING *Once* TYPE *English rose* SCENT *Strong myrrh*

CULTIVAR *'Ausfirst'*

'Constance Spry' was David Austin's very first rose, introduced in 1961. It has large pure rose-pink flowers with an extremely strong myrrh fragrance, which until that time was practically unknown. Can be grown as a large shrub, although it works much better as a climber, when it will make a most impressive and beautiful show.

Gertrude Jekyll

HEIGHT *1.5m (5ft); or 3m (10ft) as climber* SPREAD *1m (3ft)*

FLOWERING *Repeat* TYPE *English rose*

SCENT *Strong old rose* CULTIVAR *'Ausbord'*

Of all roses, 'Gertrude Jekyll' is one of the very best for fragrance – a strong, classic and delicious old rose type. The blooms are lovely – quite large and pure pink, the petals arranged in the form of a rosette. As a medium-sized shrub, it is lovely mixed up with other plants. It also makes an excellent climber (p.172).

'Gertrude Jekyll'

Hansa

HEIGHT *2m (6ft)*   SPREAD *1.5m (5ft)*
FLOWERING *Repeat*   TYPE *Rugosa hybrid*
SCENT *Strong old rose*

The rugosa roses are well-known for being particularly tough and winter hardy, bearing large hips, and having a delicious fragrance. 'Hansa' is excellent on all those counts. The double flowers are a bright magenta-pink and are followed by large red hips. The old rose fragrance is strong and delicious. A big, thorny rose that is wonderful in a hedge or a mixed border.

'Hansa'

'Lady Emma Hamilton'

Lady Emma Hamilton

HEIGHT *1m (3ft)* SPREAD *1m (3ft)*
FLOWERING *Repeat* TYPE *English rose*
SCENT *Strong fruity* CULTIVAR *'Ausbrother'*

A delicious fragrance to put a smile on your face! It is made up of a rich mix of fruits – citrus with strong hints of pear and grape, and sometimes even guava and lychee. 'Lady Emma Hamilton' is also notable for the dark bronzy colour of its leaves, especially when young. The blooms are cup-shaped and a lovely mix of rich tangerine orange on the inside of the petals and orange-yellow on the reverse. It can sometimes require a little extra care and attention to keep it growing and flowering well.

Königin von Dänemark

HEIGHT *1.5m (5ft)* SPREAD *1m (3ft)* FLOWERING *Once*
TYPE *Alba* SCENT *Strong old rose*

One of the most beautiful of the old roses, also known as 'Queen of Denmark'. The pure soft pink flowers, the colour deepening in the centre where the petals are packed together, are quartered with a central button eye. They are beautifully set off by grey-green leaves. The classic old rose fragrance is particularly delicious. The growth is quite upright if pruned each winter, but becomes more spreading and arching otherwise. A tough and reliable rose.

'Königin von Dänemark'

Rambling Rector

HEIGHT *8m (26ft)* SPREAD *5m (16ft)*
FLOWERING *Once* TYPE *Rambler*
SCENT *Strong musk*

One of the best known of the ramblers, partly because of its name but also because it is a very good rose. When in flower the leaves are barely visible because of the mass of semi-double, white flowers. The combined strength of the fragrance of so many thousands of flowers is impressive and can be detected from some distance away. Many small orange hips follow the flowers. 'Rambling Rector' is extremely vigorous and needs to be sited with care, preferably to grow up a large tree (p.200). The equally large 'Seagull' is similar, if not identical, and they are often mixed up by nurseries.

Quatre Saisons

HEIGHT *2m (6ft)* SPREAD *1.5m (5ft)*
FLOWERING *Repeat* TYPE *Damask*
SCENT *Strong old rose*

'Quatre Saisons' is also known as the autumn damask rose; and as *R. × damascena* var. *bifera* or *semperflorens*. As its names suggest, it repeat flowers – almost unheard of for a rose dating back to around 1660. The flowers are loosely double and a pure rose-pink. Robert Calkin, the rose fragrance expert, said if sunshine had a fragrance it would be like this rose. It is not the tidiest of shrubs but surrounding it with perennials would help to disguise this weak point.

The Ancient Mariner

HEIGHT *1.2m (4ft)* SPREAD *1.2m (4ft)*
FLOWERING *Repeat* TYPE *English rose*
SCENT *Medium to strong myrrh* CULTIVAR *'Ausoutcry'*

'The Ancient Mariner' is probably the best of the English roses with a myrrh fragrance. The flowers are very much in the classic old rose style, with about 160 petals beautifully arranged inside the cup-shaped outer petals, the colour being a pure rose-pink fading a little towards the outside. It is a healthy, well-mannered, bushy, and quite upright shrub that flowers freely and regularly from early until late in the season.

Madame Legras de Saint Germain

HEIGHT *2m (6ft); or 2.5m (8ft) as a climber*
SPREAD *1.5m (5ft)* FLOWERING *Once*
TYPE *Alba* SCENT *Strong old rose*

Rather a mystery rose, its parentage is not known and it is not clear to which group it really belongs. It is nevertheless a worthwhile addition to the garden, especially as good roses with white flowers are scarce. The blooms are double, with many petals spiralling round a central eye. It can be grown as a rather lax shrub or better as a climber, and has the added attribute of being thornless.

'Rambling Rector'

'The Ancient Mariner'

'Quatre Saisons'

'Madame Legras de Saint Germain'

Roses for cutting

Being able to cut roses for the house is one of
the great delights of growing them. Garden
roses may not last as long as florists' ones, but
they have much more character and fragrance.
With choices ranging from wild roses to
hybrid teas, they will work in just about any
style of arrangement.

'Queen of Sweden'

Queen of Sweden

HEIGHT *1.2m (4ft)* SPREAD *1m (3ft)* FLOWERING *Repeat*
TYPE *English rose* SCENT *Medium myrrh* CULTIVAR *'Austiger'*

The English roses are generally known for their bushy, sometimes lax growth which can make beautiful, relaxed flower arrangements, but if you want one with stiffer, straighter stems, 'Queen of Sweden' is the best choice. The petals are arranged tightly in the form of a neat rosette which starts as a soft peach and gradually changes to pale pink. The fragrance is rather variable but at its best is a good myrrh. This is a narrow, upright shrub, and to create a show is best planted in a small group. Also a good choice for a hedge (p.164).

Rosa glauca

HEIGHT *2m (6ft)* SPREAD *1.5m (5ft)* FLOWERING *Once*
TYPE *Species rose* SCENT *Little or none*

While the flowers of *Rosa glauca* are pretty and are certainly effective in arrangements, it is the rose's young growth – with plum-purple to slate-grey leaves – that is more valued by florists. The stems are also attractive purple with a white bloom. If you want to encourage these young stems, you will need to prune at least part of it hard each winter. It also bears an excellent crop of bright-red hips in autumn.

Roald Dahl

HEIGHT *1m (3ft)* SPREAD *1m (3ft)* FLOWERING *Repeat*
TYPE *English rose* SCENT *Medium tea* CULTIVAR *'Ausowlish'*

A lovely rose for making relaxed arrangements. In contrast to the orange-red buds, the open flowers are pure apricot. They are medium-sized, don't have too many petals, and so aren't too heavy, making them easier to arrange. In the vase, as in the garden, the flowers will blend beautifully with a wide range of other colours, but are especially effective with lilacs and lavenders. 'Roald Dahl' has a lovely tea fragrance and is very healthy.

Rosa glauca

'Roald Dahl'

155

Chandos Beauty

HEIGHT *1.2m (4ft)*
SPREAD *1m (3ft)*
FLOWERING *Repeat*
TYPE *Hybrid tea* SCENT *Strong sweet*
CULTIVAR *'Harmisty'*

'Chandos Beauty' is an excellent
choice for a classic hybrid tea flower
in arrangements. The blooms have
the high-pointed centre along with
a strong and delicious fragrance.
The colour is a lovely mix of amber-
gold and cream with occasional pink
flushes. The plant is strong and
robust with dark, disease-resistant
leaves. It works equally well in a
formal bed or a mixed border.

Lynda Bellingham

HEIGHT *75cm (2½ft)*
SPREAD *75cm (2½ft)*
FLOWERING *Repeat*
TYPE *Hybrid tea*
SCENT *Strong spice*
CULTIVAR *'Harwise'*

Soft pink buds change to peach as
this flower opens up. Each bloom
has about 50 petals, so the colour
is intensified in the centre where the
petals are very close to each other. It
makes a fairly short but sturdy and
healthy bush that, with its strong
fragrance, would be a very good
choice for the edge of a border or
in pots. The flowers last well both
on the bush and in arrangements.

"Consider every stage of a rose: the
bud is often a quite different colour
to the open flower, which may change
dramatically again as it fades."

Pride of England

HEIGHT *1m (3ft)*
SPREAD *60cm (2ft)*
FLOWERING *Repeat*
TYPE *Hybrid tea*   SCENT *Medium*
CULTIVAR *'Harencore'*

A classic red hybrid tea rose. The fragrant flowers are borne on stiff stems and are very large – 12cm (4in) across – and a dark red, making them a good choice for more formal arrangements or for giving to a loved one. The bush is vigorous and will quickly replace any stems taken for cutting. It may need some protection from cold winter winds.

Athena

HEIGHT *1m (3ft)*
SPREAD *60cm (2ft)*
FLOWERING *Repeat*
TYPE *Hybrid tea*   SCENT *Medium*
CULTIVAR *'Korcripoco'*

A large-flowered fragrant rose, ideal for more formal arrangements. The flowers are creamy white at first with pink on the outer edge, which gradually spreads over the whole bloom. The pink varies in intensity depending on the weather, ensuring that no two flowers are identical. They last well both in the garden and in the vase. 'Athena' is healthy and very winter hardy.

Buxom Beauty

HEIGHT *75cm (2½ft)*
SPREAD *45cm (1½ft)*
FLOWERING *Repeat*
TYPE *Hybrid tea*
SCENT *Strong sweet floral*
CULTIVAR *'Korbilant'*

As the name suggests, this rose has large flowers up to 15cm (6in) across. These have a powerful, delicious, and well-balanced fragrance, among the strongest of all roses. The deep-pink blooms are classically hybrid tea in form, and make an impressive addition to a bouquet of flowers.

'James L. Austin'

'Silas Marner'

James L. Austin

HEIGHT *1.2m (4ft)*   SPREAD *1m (3ft)*
FLOWERING *Repeat*   TYPE *English rose*
SCENT *Light to medium fruity*   CULTIVAR *'Auspike'*

In form, the flowers of 'James L. Austin' are much like those of the Portland 'Jacques Cartier', with many petals beautifully arranged around a central button eye. The colour, however, is several shades darker – a deep pink. The growth is quite bushy. A healthy rose, good in all parts of the garden. With its fruity fragrance, it is lovely in an arrangement.

Silas Marner

HEIGHT *1m (3ft)*   SPREAD *1.4m (4½ft)*   FLOWERING *Repeat*
TYPE *English rose*   SCENT *Medium to strong old rose*
CULTIVAR *'Ausraveloe'*

With its arching stems, 'Silas Marner' looks lovely in more informal arrangements mixed in with other flowers. Likewise, in the garden, this is a good choice for a mixed border. The medium-sized, cup-shaped flowers are soft pink, paler towards the outside and on the undersides of the petals. The medium-strong old rose fragrance has hints of fruity lemon, green banana, and apricot. A very healthy rose.

'Lampion'

Roses for
hips, leaves
& thorns

Roses aren't just about flowers. Some have
fragrant leaves, while others are prized for
their hips, which come in a variety of sizes,
shapes, and colours, and often last through
autumn and well into winter. There is even
one variety grown for its eye-catching thorns,
which look wonderful when backlit.

"Rose hips come
in a wide variety
of shapes, sizes,
and colours,
and are of huge
value to wildlife."

'Tottering-by-Gently'

Lampion

HEIGHT *2m (6ft)*   SPREAD *2m (6ft)*   FLOWERING *Once*
TYPE *Species rose*   SCENT *Light*   CULTIVAR *'Tan06004'*

Also known as the chestnut rose, this is an extremely distinctive variety, prized for its flowers as well as its hips. Its common name comes from the similarity of the spiny hips to the fruit of the horse chestnut. This form of *Rosa roxburghii* has the advantage of having orange-yellow hips that remain on the plant for much longer than those of the original species. The flowers are large and soft pink with a white centre.

Tottering-by-Gently

HEIGHT *1.2m (4ft)*   SPREAD *1.2m (4ft)*   FLOWERING *Repeat*
TYPE *English rose*   SCENT *Light to medium musk*
CULTIVAR *'Auscartoon'*

The majority of roses that set a good crop of hips are large, often 2m (6ft) or more, and tricky to fit into smaller gardens. 'Tottering-by-Gently', on the other hand, is medium-sized and its single yellow flowers look good in a mixed border. If not dead-headed, it produces a heavy crop of medium-sized orange hips in early autumn that last through the winter. A very good, tough, and reliable rose.

Rosa sericea subsp. *omeiensis* f. *pteracantha*

HEIGHT *2.5m (8ft)*   SPREAD *2m (6ft)*   FLOWERING *Once*
TYPE *Species rose*   SCENT *Little or none*

When seen with the sun shining through them, the large, broad, blood-red thorns of this rose (also known as *R. omeiensis* 'Pteracantha') make a brilliant show. They are only red in the first year, so to ensure a good supply of young stems the rose should be pruned quite heavily each year. The flowers, which are only produced on older stems, are small, white, and only have four petals. The hips are small and bright red, but drop off as soon as they are ripe.

Rosa sericea subsp. *omeiensis* f. *pteracantha*

'William Lobb'

Rosa rubiginosa

HEIGHT *2.5m (8ft); often more* SPREAD *2.5m (8ft); often more* FLOWERING *Once* TYPE *Species rose* SCENT *Light to medium*

The sweet briar (also known as *R. eglantaria*, or eglantine) is native to the British Isles and much of Europe. It is similar to the dog rose, although the flowers are a little darker and the stems much more thorny (indeed ferociously so). The flowers are followed by shiny, rich-red oval hips which last into the winter. After rain, or if crushed lightly, the young leaves smell just like green apples. For the best fragrance, you'll need to keep cutting the stems back, although this will mean no flowers or hips unless you leave a few to keep growing. It thrives on alkaline soils.

Rosa rubiginosa

William Lobb

HEIGHT *2.5m (8ft)*   SPREAD *1.5m (5ft)*
FLOWERING *Once*   TYPE *Moss rose*   SCENT *Strong*

'William Lobb' is one of the most disease-resistant of the moss roses. It has large dark-crimson flowers that turn a shade of lavender as they age. These are strongly fragrant, and the "moss" also has a delicious, resinous smell. Leave 'William Lobb' unpruned to form a climber – it will grow 3–4m (10–13ft) up into a tree, for instance – or keep it pruned as a shrub, 1.5–2m (5–6ft) tall.

Scarlet Fire

HEIGHT *3m (10ft)*   SPREAD *2m (6ft)*   FLOWERING *Once*
TYPE *Modern shrub*   SCENT *Light*

While 'Scarlet Fire' (or 'Scharlachglut') only flowers once, in midsummer, it has another season of striking beauty when its large, pear-shaped, orange-red hips are produced. It makes a large shrub and so is best at the back of a border or in a wild area. A spring or late-summer flowering clematis could be grown up it to make its season of interest even longer.

Rosa rugosa 'Alba'

HEIGHT *1.2m (4ft)*   SPREAD *1.2m (4ft)*   FLOWERING *Repeat*
TYPE *Species rose*   SCENT *Strong old rose*

The hips of both this rose and the original pink form of *Rosa rugosa* are bright red, shiny, and the size of cherry tomatoes. They follow wide-open single white flowers that are produced over a long season, from early summer to late autumn, a rare feature in wild roses. *Rosa rugosa* grows on the coasts of northern Japan, North Korea, Siberia, and northeastern China, and so is incredibly tough and winter hardy. In garden situations its thorny stems make it useful for making an impenetrable hedge. It will also thrive in spots where the soil is poor and little else will grow, and is equally effective in a mixed border. It is completely disease-resistant.

'Scarlet Fire'

Rosa rugosa 'Alba'

'The Generous Gardener'

Rosa spinosissima

The Generous Gardener

HEIGHT *2m (6ft); or 4m (13ft) as a climber*
SPREAD *3m (10ft)* FLOWERING *Repeat*
TYPE *Climbing English rose* SCENT *Strong old rose,
musk and myrrh* CULTIVAR *'Ausdrawn'*

A wonderful climber that, if not dead-headed, will bear a superb crop of large orange-red hips that last right through the winter. Allowing the hips to grow may reduce the number of flowers produced later in the season, but it is a sacrifice worth making. The flowers are large, loosely double, and blush pink, paling with age. They open to look charmingly like waterlilies and have a most delicious fragrance. 'The Generous Gardener' can be grown as a large arching shrub, but is better trained as a climber. The young leaves are a bright bronze colour and stay very healthy.

Rosa spinosissima

HEIGHT *1m (3ft) (often less)* SPREAD *Indefinite – spreads
by suckers* FLOWERING *Once* TYPE *Species rose*
SCENT *Medium to strong*

Known as the Scotch or burnet rose, and also as *R. pimpinellifolia*, this and some of its hybrids are the only roses to bear black hips. Its leaves have many small, dark leaflets. The flowers are single and creamy white and have a delicious fragrance. An incredibly tough rose, it is very low-growing in the wild, where it even grows on sand dunes, but gets taller in better soils.

Geranium

HEIGHT *2.5m (8ft)* SPREAD *2.5m (8ft)*
FLOWERING *Once* TYPE *Species rose* SCENT *Light*

Also known as *Rosa moyesii* 'Geranium', this may well be the best-known rose for hips. They don't last all that long, but they are striking – pendulous, flagon-shaped, and bright vermillion-red. The single flowers are the same shade of red, enhanced by yellow stamens. It is a big rose, so needs to be planted where there is room for it to reach its full potential.

'Geranium'

Roses for hedges

Roses can be grown in every style and height of hedge, from short and formal to tall and impenetrable. Rose hedges are colourful and fragrant, and can be a valuable source of food and shelter for a wide variety of wildlife.

The Lark Ascending

HEIGHT *2m (6ft)* SPREAD *1.5m (5ft)* FLOWERING *Repeat*
TYPE *English rose* SCENT *Light tea/myrrh*
CULTIVAR *'Ausursula'*

This lovely light and airy rose will mark a boundary without completely obscuring the view beyond. With only a few petals the flowers are airy too, and are a soft apricot, paling with age. This is a good rose for bees. It is extremely healthy and, unusually for a rose of this colour, very winter hardy.

Queen of Sweden

HEIGHT *1.2m (4ft)* SPREAD *1m (3ft)*
FLOWERING *Repeat* TYPE *English rose*
SCENT *Medium myrrh* CULTIVAR *'Austiger'*

With its upright, rather narrow growth, 'Queen of Sweden' is perfect for a neat, internal boundary in a garden. The flowers are neat too – upward-facing, medium-sized rosettes that start a soft apricot before slowly changing to soft pink as they age. The fragrance, though not strong, is a soft and particularly delicious myrrh. 'Queen of Sweden' repeat-flowers well and is very healthy.

'The Lark Ascending'

'Queen of Sweden'

Crème Chantilly

HEIGHT *75cm (1½ft)*
SPREAD *1m (3ft)*
FLOWERING *Repeat*
TYPE *Modern shrub*
SCENT *None*
CULTIVAR *'Meiradena'*

This rose's small, pretty, cup-shaped flowers start a soft creamy colour, turning to pure white, and are set off by grey-green foliage. 'Crème Chantilly' makes a short, rounded shrub that makes a good choice for a low hedge. It is also very winter hardy and extremely healthy, and has won several awards in Europe.

Goldspatz

HEIGHT *1.5m (5ft)*
SPREAD *1m (3ft)*
FLOWERING *Repeat*
TYPE *Modern shrub*
SCENT *None or light*
CULTIVAR *'Korgellan'*

An extremely healthy, winter-hardy and weather-resistant rose with attractive, arching stems. The flowers are semi-double, quite small, and produced in great profusion; bees love them. They are soft yellow fading to a rich cream. Its informal character makes 'Goldspatz' a wonderful choice for a boundary hedge, although it is equally good inside the garden. It does well in semi-shady situations.

Île de Fleurs

HEIGHT *1.2m (4ft)*
SPREAD *75cm (2½ft)*
FLOWERING *Repeat*
TYPE *Floribunda*
SCENT *Medium to strong musk*

An award-winning rose with outstanding health. Its growth is bushy but quite upright, 'Île de Fleurs' is excellent for a hedge. The violet-purple flowers are semi-double, and the petals drop cleanly, always useful when multiples are planted. The fragrance is a fairly strong musk. The flowers are followed by a good crop of small hips. 'Île de Fleurs' creates a strong focal point in a mixed border.

Kew Gardens

HEIGHT *1.2m (4ft)*
SPREAD *1.2m (4ft)*
FLOWERING *Repeat*
TYPE *English rose*
SCENT *Little or none*
CULTIVAR *'Ausfence'*

'Kew Gardens' makes a first-class hedging rose. It produces its single white flowers incredibly freely from the ground up and it repeats extremely well. It has the great advantage of being completely thornless – useful when mowing close to it. It is also an effective rose in mixed borders. A very healthy variety.

Thomas à Becket

HEIGHT *1.5m (5ft)*
SPREAD *1.2m (4ft)*
FLOWERING *Repeat*
TYPE *English rose*
SCENT *Medium old rose*
CULTIVAR *'Auswinston'*

Good red roses suitable for hedges are difficult to find, with 'Thomas à Becket' being a rare exception. It is closely related to wild roses, giving it a distinctive appearance. Its growth is quite upright but very bushy, and eventually slightly arching. The bright crimson flowers start as shallow cups, before opening to informal rosettes, the outer petals reflexing back. It makes a showy and substantial hedge.

Pink Roadrunner

HEIGHT *75cm (2½ft)*
SPREAD *75cm (2½ft)*
FLOWERING *Repeat*
TYPE *Rugosa hybrid*
SCENT *Strong old rose*
CULTIVAR *'Uhlarium'*

Being a rugosa hybrid usually means that a rose will be tough, disease-resistant and winter hardy, and this is all true of 'Pink Roadrunner'. The flowers vary from semi-double to double and are a pure rose pink. They are produced freely from early summer to late in the year. It makes a good hedge, although it works well in other parts of the garden, too.

Olivia Rose Austin

HEIGHT *1.2m (4ft)* SPREAD *1m (3ft)*
FLOWERING *Repeat* TYPE *English rose* SCENT *Light to medium fruity* CULTIVAR *'Ausmixture'*

Any rose chosen for a hedge, or any other kind of mass planting, needs to be especially healthy, and 'Olivia Rose Austin' is ideal. It also has a long flowering season, starting about two to three weeks before most others and then repeating very quickly. The soft-pink flowers are big, with many petals beautifully arranged in a rosette.

Harlow Carr

HEIGHT *1m (3ft)* SPREAD *1m (3ft)*
FLOWERING *Repeat* TYPE *English rose*
SCENT *Medium to strong old rose* CULTIVAR *'Aushouse'*

'Harlow Carr' is extremely thorny, with stems that arch over and intermingle to make an excellent, impenetrable hedge. The flowers are medium-sized, rose-pink, and deliciously fragrant. A very healthy rose that could be planted in a number of places in the garden, both formal and informal.

'Harlow Carr'

'Olivia Rose Austin'

168

Roses for
warm, sunny
walls

Although all roses need at least a few
hours of sun a day, the plants featured here are
real sun-worshippers. They'll appreciate good soil
and regular watering, and reward you with an
abundance of flowers and plenty of perfume.

'The Lady of the Lake'

The Lady of the Lake

HEIGHT *4m (13ft)* SPREAD *3m (10ft)* FLOWERING *Repeat*
TYPE *Rambler* SCENT *Medium fruity* CULTIVAR *'Ausherbert'*

Most ramblers are too vigorous to grow up walls and fences,
but 'The Lady of the Lake' is an exception. The flowers are
typically small but they are produced continuously from
early summer through to early winter. They vary in colour
between soft pink and soft apricot and do not have too many
petals, so bees can easily access the many stamens. 'The Lady
of the Lake' is also ideal for pergolas and arches. A very
healthy variety with attractive leaves and dark stems,
especially when young.

Climbing Étoile de Hollande

HEIGHT *4m (13ft)* SPREAD *2.5m (8ft)* FLOWERING *Repeat*
TYPE *Hybrid tea* SCENT *Strong old rose*

'Étoile de Hollande' is one of the very best roses for scent. It
is powerful and delicious – a rich, sweet old rose fragrance.
The rich, velvety crimson flowers are a little formless when
fully out, but a classic hybrid tea shape at first. This is a
vigorous climber and needs plenty of space, although the
long stems are quite easy to fan out. It will set a good crop of
large red hips if not dead-headed. It is a little susceptible
to black spot, but with some extra care and attention it is a
wonderful rose to have in the garden.

The Generous Gardener

HEIGHT *4m (13ft)* SPREAD *3m (10ft)* FLOWERING *Repeat*
TYPE *English rose* SCENT *Strong old rose, tea, myrrh*
CULTIVAR *'Ausdrawn'*

'The Generous Gardener' was initially introduced as a large
shrub, but it soon became evident that it is more successful as
a climber. It is perhaps best trained against a wall where its
long, quite stiff stems can be fanned out, but it is also excellent
on an arbour or pergola where its wonderful fragrance can be
appreciated. The flowers are large and a pure, soft pink, with
a delicious mix of old rose, myrrh, and tea fragrances. If not
dead-headed it will set a good crop of large orange-red hips.

'Climbing Étoile de Hollande'

'The Generous Gardener'

Ghislaine de Féligonde

HEIGHT *3m (10ft)* SPREAD *2m (6ft)* FLOWERING *Repeat*
TYPE *Rambler* SCENT *Medium musky*

A rose introduced over 100 years ago, whose qualities
and garden worthiness have only recently been
recognized. It can be grown as a large arching shrub,
but its almost thornless stems and medium vigour make
it ideal for a fence. As long as it is well watered, the heat
from a sunny wall will encourage more flowers. These
are small, double, and vary greatly in colour between
soft apricot and pink. A tough and reliable rose.

Gertrude Jekyll

HEIGHT *2.5m (8ft)* SPREAD *2m (6ft)*
FLOWERING *Repeat* TYPE *English Rose*
SCENT *Strong old rose* CULTIVAR *'Ausbord'*

With its relatively stiff, upright growth, 'Gertrude
Jekyll' is an excellent choice for growing against a fence
or wall. The stems can either be left to grow vertically
or gently fanned out to encourage more flowers and
better coverage. The blooms are large, with petals
beautifully arranged in a rosette, and are a strong, pure
pink. The crowning glory of this rose, though, is its
superb old rose fragrance. Wonderful to frame a door or
for training over an arch.

'Gertrude Jekyll'

'Ghislaine de Féligonde'

Climbing Lady Hillingdon

HEIGHT *4m (13ft)* SPREAD *3m (10ft)*
FLOWERING *Repeat* TYPE *Tea*
SCENT *Strong fruity tea*

Tea roses love the heat and are generally not very successful in cooler climates like that of the UK, but if you can train 'Lady Hillingdon' up a warm, sunny wall it will be very happy and continue to flower with great regularity through summer and into autumn. The flowers are beautifully shaped, long and pointed, and the colour is a rich apricot-yellow. They emit a strong and delicious fruity tea fragrance. They are set off by dark-green leaves which are dark crimson when young, as are the young stems. With its supple growth, this is an easy rose to fan out on a wall, although it is important to give it the space it requires.

Golden Gate

HEIGHT *3m (10ft)* SPREAD *2m (6ft)*
FLOWERING *Repeat* TYPE *Climber*
SCENT *Medium sweet fruity*
CULTIVAR *'Korgolgat'*

An extremely healthy variety that will stand out in every situation in the garden. The flowers are large, up to 10cm (4in) across, and a bright golden yellow. They have a particularly delicious fruity fragrance – citrus with a strong element of tropical flowers. 'Golden Gate' is especially good for walls and fences, even if they're partly shady. The growth is not too stiff, and can be trained over an arch.

Madame Plantier

HEIGHT *3m (10ft)*
SPREAD *2.5m (8ft)*
FLOWERING *Once* TYPE *Alba*
SCENT *Strong sweet old rose*

A beautiful rose that sadly is not often seen, probably just because it doesn't repeat-flower. The small buds are soft pink but open to perfectly white, medium-sized, full-petalled flowers, with the petals perfectly arranged around a little green eye. The fragrance is delicious and strong. With its slim, thornless, arching stems, it can be grown as a rounded shrub, but is perhaps better trained up a wall, fence, or obelisk, or planted to scramble into a small tree. It's a noisette/alba cross that combines the hardiness of an alba with a noisette's ability to grow in hot climates.

Climbing Mrs Herbert Stevens

HEIGHT *5m (16ft)* SPREAD *3m (10ft)*
FLOWERING *Repeat*
TYPE *Hybrid tea* SCENT *Strong tea*

First introduced as a climber back in 1922, the excellence of this variety is proven by its age, given how few roses from that time are still grown today. In fact it was initially bred as a bush rose in 1910; a sport from that produced this climbing form. Both have the most beautiful blooms with the classic high-point centre of the hybrid teas, although more refined than many more modern varieties. The large flowers are pure white except for a slight yellow tint at the centre. They hang down, which is a disadvantage on a bush but a bonus on a climber. The fragrance is particularly strong and delicious. This is a vigorous climber, and the stems are quite stiff too – so it needs plenty of space.

Lavender Siluetta

HEIGHT *2m (6ft)* SPREAD *1m (3ft)*
FLOWERING *Repeat*
TYPE *Climber*
SCENT *Light to medium sweet and spicy*
CULTIVAR *'Korsilu09'*

The beautifully simple, almost single flowers of this rose are produced very freely throughout the season from early summer through to beginning of winter. They are a lovely soft shade of lavender-pink, paling with age to create a subtle mix of colours. 'Lavender Siluetta' isn't too vigorous and its stems are flexible – easy to fan out on a short wall or twine around an obelisk (p.188). If tightly pruned it also makes an excellent hedge.

Roses for semi-shady walls

North-facing walls and those in partial shade are always a bit of a challenge for climbing plants, but there are quite a few roses that will do well on them, as long as they get at least four hours of direct sun. The shade will help to prevent the blooms from scorching and make them last longer.

'Hella'

Hella

HEIGHT *2.5m (8ft)*   SPREAD *1m (3ft)*
FLOWERING *Repeat*   TYPE *Climber*
SCENT *Light*   CULTIVAR *'Korditwol'*

'Hella' is similar to the popular floribunda 'Iceberg' but with much better health. The flowers are pure white and semi-double, with plenty of stamens showing in the middle. It is free-flowering, and its flexible stems make it easy to train on a wall or over an arch or pergola. A healthy, award-winning rose.

Madame Alfred Carrière

HEIGHT *5m (16ft)*   SPREAD *3m (10ft)*
FLOWERING *Repeat*   TYPE *Noisette climber*
SCENT *Strong fruit*

'Madame Alfred' is popular around the world, since it's tolerant of a wide range of climates as well as positions in the garden. It's a vigorous variety that needs lots of space. The flower buds are pale pink, turning white as soon as they open. They are not particularly shapely but are produced in large quantities and have a deliciously sweet, often strongly grapefruit fragrance. Noisettes are usually a little on the tender side and require sun, but this one is hardy, and grows and flowers well in a certain amount of shade. It is best trained against a wall, which is made easier by the fact that it is nearly thornless, although this makes it less suitable for growing into a tree.

'Madame Alfred Carrière'

'City of York'

'Leverkusen'

City of York

HEIGHT *5m (16ft)* SPREAD *3m (10ft)*
FLOWERING *Once, with a few later* TYPE *Wichurana rambler*
SCENT *Light to medium musk, citrus*

Also known as 'Direktör Benschop', the pure white flowers of this rose make it good for brightening up a shady spot. The flowers are semi-double, with prominent golden-yellow stamens making them attractive to bees. They are set off by dark-green, healthy leaves. Also grows well on a sunny wall, pergola, or good-sized arch.

Chevy Chase

HEIGHT *4m (13ft)* SPREAD *3m (10ft)* FLOWERING *Once*
TYPE *Rambler* SCENT *Light or none*

This is probably the best dark-crimson rambler, the small flowers being very neat and perfectly formed. They are produced profusely a little later than most roses but then keep their colour for a long time. It works well grown up a small tree or large shrub. An extremely healthy rose.

Leverkusen

HEIGHT *3m (10ft)* SPREAD *2m (6ft)* FLOWERING *Repeat*
TYPE *Climber* SCENT *Medium fruit*

'Leverkusen' was introduced in 1954 and was the first of a group called the Kordesii Hybrids, bred for great winter hardiness and disease resistance. It is still highly regarded today and has attractive, quite large, yellow flowers – deeper in colour in the middle, much softer on the outside. They are followed by hips that stay green for a long time, eventually turning yellow. 'Leverkusen' makes a bushy climber tolerant of shade. It could also be grown as a large shrub.

‘Chevy Chase’

‘Chawton Cottage’

Chawton Cottage

HEIGHT *2.5m (8ft)* SPREAD *2m (6ft)*
FLOWERING *Repeat* TYPE *Climber* SCENT *Light*
CULTIVAR *‘Harzimlet’*

From its *Rosa persica* parentage, ‘Chawton Cottage’ has the distinguishing feature of a dark ruby-red eye at the base of its pearly-pink petals. As it is not too vigorous it is perfect for a short wall or fence, or for an arch. It is free-flowering and repeats well. The leaves are a dark glossy green and very healthy. A tough rose.

Purple Skyliner

HEIGHT *2.5m (8ft)* SPREAD *2m (6ft)*
FLOWERING *Repeat* TYPE *Rambler*
SCENT *Medium* CULTIVAR *'Franwekpurp'*

A small climber with semi-double, soft-purple flowers that fade to mauve and grey. They look similar to those of the vigorous, once-flowering rambler 'Veilchenblau', but 'Purple Skyliner' flowers freely, repeats well, and is easy to manage. It also makes a lovely shrub, and is good for growing on an obelisk (p.185).

The Pilgrim

HEIGHT *3m (10ft)* SPREAD *2m (6ft)*
FLOWERING *Repeat* TYPE *Climbing English rose*
SCENT *Medium tea and myrrh* CULTIVAR *'Auswalker'*

'The Pilgrim' has been growing on an open but north-facing wall at David Austin Roses for many years, and every year looks absolutely superb. It is pruned fairly lightly and has eventually reached right up to the gutters of a two-story building, although it could easily be kept shorter. The yellow flowers will brighten up any wall, the 140 petals being perfectly arranged in a rosette.

James Galway

HEIGHT *3m (10ft)* SPREAD *2m (6ft)*
FLOWERING *Repeat* TYPE *Climbing English rose*
SCENT *Light to medium old rose* CULTIVAR *'Auscrystal'*

After initially being introduced as a shrub, it soon became evident that 'James Galway' is much better grown as a climber. It has large flowers tightly packed with about 130 very weather-resistant petals. These are a lovely warm pink in the centre, paling to blush at the edges. The stems have few thorns and are quite stiff, but can still be fanned out on a 2m (6ft) high wall or fence.

Climbing Madame Caroline Testout

HEIGHT *5m (16ft)* SPREAD *2.5m (8ft)*
FLOWERING *Some repeat* TYPE *Climbing hybrid tea*
SCENT *Medium sweet*

With its large silvery-pink, rather rounded flowers and rolled-back petals, 'Madame Caroline Testout' is a distinctive rose. Its growth is quite stiff and prickly – not the easiest to fan out. It's important therefore to give it a good-sized wall, 4–5m (13–16ft) high, to grow on. The flowers last a long time on the plant but luckily the petals drop off cleanly. This climbing form originated from a bush that was planted in huge quantities along sidewalks in Portland, Oregon. It is healthy, tough, reliable, and extremely long-lived, often lasting 100 years or more.

'Purple Skyliner'

'James Galway'

'The Pilgrim'

'Climbing Madame Caroline Testout'

Roses for
arches, pergolas,
obelisks & pillars

These structures are a great way to feature climbing roses within
your garden. Arches need varieties that flower from the ground up
and are flexible enough to be tied down to grow over them. Pergolas
are good with a combination of climbers on their pillars and some
ramblers that can be trained horizontally along the top. Upright,
tall shrubs are good for pillars and obelisks.

'Narrow Water'

Narrow Water

HEIGHT *2.5m (8ft)* SPREAD *2m (6ft)* FLOWERING *Repeat*
TYPE *Climbing noisette* SCENT *Medium to strong musk*

The pretty little flowers are produced in great profusion right
to the end of the season. The pink buds open to semi-double
mauve blooms that fade to cream and white, giving a lovely
mix of colours. It has the musky clove fragrance typical
of noisettes. Good for growing over an arch, through
a small tree, or as a tall shrub if kept pruned. Unusually hardy
for a noisette.

Scent from Heaven

HEIGHT *3m (10ft)* SPREAD *2m (6ft)* FLOWERING *Repeat*
TYPE *Patio climber* SCENT *Strong fruit* CULTIVAR *'Chewbabaluv'*

This rose is both wonderfully fragrant (rare in patio climbers)
and richly coloured. The apricot-pink flowers are medium-
sized and produced freely from the ground upwards. The
leaves are glossy and disease-resistant.

Malvern Hills

HEIGHT *4m (13ft)* SPREAD *3m (10ft)*
FLOWERING *Repeat* TYPE *English rose rambler*
SCENT *Light to medium musk* CULTIVAR *'Auscanary'*

A lovely and versatile rose. The abundant flowers are quite
small, turning from buff to yellow then cream. The petals are
in a rosette formation with, initially at least, a little button
eye. 'Malvern Hills' is vigorous enough to cover a pergola
quickly, but without becoming a menace.

'Scent from Heaven'

'Malvern Hills'

Paul Noël

HEIGHT *4m (13ft)* SPREAD *3m (10ft)* FLOWERING *Some repeating* TYPE *Rambler* SCENT *Medium tea/fruit*

A rather unusual rambler resulting from an interesting cross between the wild rose R. *wichurana* and the tea rose 'Monsieur Tillier'. It was widely grown as 'Paul Transon' in the UK, until the confusion with the similar 'Paul Noël' was recognized. The large size and the colour – soft salmon-pink, quickly paling – come from its tea parent. The first flowering in early summer is generous, and is followed by a second flush later in the season, especially if the soil is kept damp. Its lax growth definitely comes from its wild rose background, and makes it perfect for growing along pergolas, or over outbuildings and trees. The fragrance is an interesting mix of apple with a hint of chrysanthemum.

Super Fairy

HEIGHT *3m (10ft)* SPREAD *2m (6ft)* FLOWERING *Repeat* TYPE *Rambler* SCENT *Light* CULTIVAR *'Helsufair'*

This is the lightest in colour of the 'Super' series bred by Karl Hetzel, who wanted to combine the abundance of the old ramblers with excellent repeat-flowering. The pink flowers are small, very double, and produced in large clusters on lax stems that can be used to encircle pillars and obelisks, or fanned out on a wall or fence. It also makes an effective weeping standard. Lovely in flower arrangements, especially as it lasts well when cut.

'Super Fairy'

'Paul Noël'

'Purple Skyliner'

Purple Skyliner

HEIGHT *2.6m (8ft)*   SPREAD *2m (6ft)*
FLOWERING *Repeat*   TYPE *Climber*
SCENT *Medium*   CULTIVAR *'Franwekpurp'*

This is an excellent choice for an obelisk or pillar. Its height is just right, it flowers profusely and continuously, and it is very healthy. The semi-double soft-purple flowers fade to grey, and have a lovely fragrance. A tough variety, 'Purple Skyliner' tolerates some shade (p.180) and poor conditions.

Allegro

HEIGHT *2m (6ft)* SPREAD *1.5m (5ft)*
FLOWERING *Repeat* TYPE *Climber*
SCENT *Light to medium*
CULTIVAR *'Meileodevin'*

A good all-round variety. The medium-sized flowers are a strong shade of rose-pink, with their many petals arranged in the same style as the old roses. 'Allegro' is healthy and repeat-flowers well. Being relatively short, makes it ideal as a balcony or patio climber, grown up an obelisk or pillar, or as a lovely arching shrub.

Jasmina

HEIGHT *2.5m (8ft)* SPREAD *1m (3ft)*
FLOWERING *Repeat* TYPE *Climber*
SCENT *Strong fruity*
CULTIVAR *'Korcentex'*

'Jasmina' is a lovely variety, with very double flowers, the petals being arranged in a quartered rosette like those of the old roses. They are medium-sized, varying in colour between violet and pink, and have a strong and delicious fragrance – fresh apple with hints of pear and apricot. 'Jasmina' produces an abundance of flowers – which are good for cutting – and repeats well. It is very winter hardy and extremely healthy.

Crown Princess Margareta

HEIGHT *3m (10ft)* SPREAD *2.5m (8ft)*
FLOWERING *Repeat* TYPE *Climbing English rose* SCENT *Strong fruity*
CULTIVAR *'Auswinter'*

A rose with wonderfully rich apricot flowers and a strong, fruity fragrance, although there is a hint of tea in there as well. The many petals are beautifully arranged in a rosette. While 'Crown Princess Margareta' can be kept as a large shrub, it is better trained as a climber, especially in warmer climates. Very healthy and winter hardy.

Warm Welcome

HEIGHT *2.5m (8ft)* SPREAD *1.5m (5ft)*
FLOWERING *Repeat*
TYPE *Patio climber* SCENT *Light*
CULTIVAR *'Chewizz'*

A particularly vivid and eye-catching rose. It produces a mass of small, nearly single flowers of bright, bright orange. They are produced continuously the whole season long, and from the ground up to the top of the plant, until the cold stops them. It is a very healthy rose, and excellent for obelisks and pillars.

Alaska

HEIGHT *2m (6ft)* SPREAD *1m (3ft)*
FLOWERING *Repeat* TYPE *Climber*
SCENT *Light to medium*
CULTIVAR *'Korjoslio'*

Really good white climbing roses are difficult to find, especially those with large, full-petalled blooms, but 'Alaska' is a fine example. It is not too vigorous, so will be easy to keep under control – an important requirement when choosing a rose for an arch. Extremely healthy and winter hardy.

Maid of Kent

HEIGHT *4m (13ft)* SPREAD *3m (10ft)*
FLOWERING *Repeat*
TYPE *Climber* SCENT *Light*

'Maid of Kent' is one of those roses that could be called a climber or a rambler. It is a worthwhile variety, producing great quantities of small semi-double, soft-pink flowers that fade to blush. Its growth is vigorous and lax, making it perfect for pergolas and growing through trees.

"Arches and pergolas work best when they serve a clear function in a garden, marking the transition from one area to the next."

'Aglaia'

Lavender Siluetta

HEIGHT *2m (6ft)* SPREAD *1m (3ft)*
FLOWERING *Repeat* TYPE *Climber* SCENT *Light to medium sweet and spicy* CULTIVAR *'Korsilu09'*

One of the great features of the roses coming from the German breeders Kordes is their excellent health. The Siluetta group are a fairly recent development, all being relatively short climbers producing generous quantities of small flowers. The flowers of 'Lavender Siluetta' are semi-double and a lovely shade of lavender, paling slightly with age. The stems are flexible, so can be spiralled around a pillar or obelisk. They can also be grown up a warm, sunny wall (p.175).

'Lavender Siluetta'

Aglaia

HEIGHT *4m (13ft)*   SPREAD *2.5m (8ft)*
FLOWERING *Once*   TYPE *Rambler*   SCENT *Strong musk*

One of the most free-flowering ramblers, and one that is sadly rarely seen. The stems are a little on the stiff side, so may well need tying down, but it is virtually thornless. The semi-double flowers start a soft yellow, fading fairly quickly to cream and white, so that when in full flower there is a whole range of colours. With its soft colouring, strong musky fragrance and good health, 'Aglaia' should be planted more often.

Sunny Siluetta

HEIGHT *2m (6ft)*   SPREAD *1m (3ft)*
FLOWERING *Repeat*   TYPE *Climber*   SCENT *Light to medium*   CULTIVAR *'Korsilu05'*

The flowers of repeat-flowering 'Sunny Siluetta' are almost single and produced prolifically over a long season. With its flexible stems it is easy to train over an arch or against a wall or fence. A healthy and very winter hardy rose.

Crimson Siluetta

HEIGHT *2m (6ft)*   SPREAD *1m (3ft)*
FLOWERING *Repeat*   TYPE *Rambler*   SCENT *Light*
CULTIVAR *'Korsilu06'*

'Crimson Siluetta' is similar to the well-known rambler 'Chevy Chase' (p.178) but it repeat-flowers well and is much less vigorous, making it ideal for obelisks and pillars. The flowers are small, fully double, pure carmine-red, and are produced freely from the ground up. 'Crimson Siluetta' can also be grown as a hedge. It is very healthy.

'Sunny Siluetta'

'Crimson Siluetta'

Summertime

HEIGHT *2.5m (8ft)*   SPREAD *1m (3ft)*
FLOWERING *Repeat*   TYPE *Patio climber*
SCENT *Medium sweet*   CULTIVAR *'Chewlarmoll'*

A cheerful little rose. The flowers are small but produced in great profusion all summer and through to the autumn. Patio climbers aren't known for their fragrance, but 'Summertime' has a sweet smell. It is a particularly tough and healthy rose, able to put up with less than ideal conditions, although it will flower much better if looked after well.

Laguna

HEIGHT *2.5m (8ft)*   SPREAD *1m (3ft)*
FLOWERING *Repeat*   TYPE *Climber*
SCENT *Strong fruity*   CULTIVAR *'Koradigel'*

A garden-worthy variety notable for its fragrance, which is particularly delicious and strong. It is a rich and well-balanced mix of different components, including fresh lemon, lychee, old rose, and patchouli! The large flowers (up to 10cm/4in across) are a pure, deep pink. 'Laguna' is an award-winning rose – healthy and extremely winter hardy. It flowers well in part shade.

Rambling Rosie

HEIGHT *2.5m (8ft)*   SPREAD *1.5m (5ft)*
FLOWERING *Repeat*   TYPE *Rambler*
SCENT *Light to medium*   CULTIVAR *'Horjasper'*

A brilliantly coloured small rambler that will repeat-flower from early summer through to late in the year. The semi-double flowers are quite small and bright crimson, with a hint of a white eye. 'Rambling Rosie' flowers prolifically from the ground up, making it perfect for pillars, obelisks, arches and, of course, walls and fences. Some nurseries also offer it as a standard, where the stems will arch gracefully down. An extremely healthy variety.

The Albrighton Rambler

HEIGHT *4m (13ft)*   SPREAD *3m (10ft)*
FLOWERING *Repeat*   TYPE *English rose rambler*
SCENT *Light musk*   CULTIVAR *'Ausmobile'*

The individual flowers of this variety are like perfect little old roses, with many petals beautifully arranged around a central darker eye. They are a soft pink (sometimes slightly apricot), paling to blush, then almost to white, and are held in large sprays on the end of long, gracefully arching stems. Not being too vigorous and with a fairly lax habit, it is quite easy to train this rose horizontally over a pergola.

'Summertime'

'Rambling Rosie'

'Laguna'

'The Albrighton Rambler'

'Mortimer Sackler'

Roses for walls & fences

A rose on a wall or fence is one of the absolute classic garden elements. With the right variety choice they can give more than any other type of climber – beautiful blooms, colour, scent, and a long flowering period. They can turn a drab wall into a beautiful one.

"Of all the ways to grow roses, training them up beside a front door is perhaps the most popular."

'Claire Austin'

Mortimer Sackler

HEIGHT *3m (10ft)* SPREAD *3m (10ft)* FLOWERING *Repeat*
TYPE *Climbing English rose* SCENT *Light to medium fruity old rose* CULTIVAR *'Ausorts'*

'Mortimer Sackler' is easy to recognize, with its medium-sized flowers and distinctive leaves and stems. The buds are rose-pink, opening up to soft pink, loosely double flowers that pale towards the outside and with age. They are beautifully set off by the dark leaves and dark, almost thornless stems. With light pruning, 'Mortimer Sackler' can exceed 3m (10ft) when grown against a warm wall, but it can also be used as a large shrub for the back of the border.

Claire Austin

HEIGHT *3m (10ft)* SPREAD *2m (6ft)* FLOWERING *Repeat*
TYPE *Climbing English rose* SCENT *Strong myrrh*
CULTIVAR *'Ausprior'*

Like red roses, good white roses are not easy to breed. 'Claire Austin', though, has large flowers and excellent health. It was first introduced as a shrub rose but its vigour soon made it plain that it is best grown as a short climber. The rounded, creamy white flowers have a strong and delicious myrrh fragrance with additional hints of meadowsweet, heliotrope, and vanilla.

Graham Thomas

HEIGHT *3m (10ft)* SPREAD *2m (6ft)* FLOWERING *Repeat*
TYPE *English rose* SCENT *Medium to strong tea*
CULTIVAR *'Ausmas'*

This is the rose that caught the attention of so many gardeners at its introduction at the Chelsea Flower Show in 1983, and was responsible for the initial popularity of David Austin's English roses. Its flowers are the richest, purest deep yellow, cupped at first, before opening to beautiful rosettes. Their fragrance is a particularly strong and delicious tea. Like many English roses, 'Graham Thomas' has the valuable characteristic of flowering from the ground up.

'Graham Thomas'

Open Arms

HEIGHT *2.5m (8ft)*
SPREAD *2m (6ft)*
FLOWERING *Repeat*
TYPE *Patio rambler*
SCENT *Light musk*
CULTIVAR *'Chewpixcel'*

The breeder of this rose, Chris Warner, introduced various patio climbers and patio ramblers. All are relatively short and compact, and so suitable for small spaces. They also have the wonderful ability to flower from the ground up. 'Open Arms' has small, almost single flowers that open salmon-pink, turning to pale pink, with a central white eye and a prominent bunch of stamens. It is very healthy and flowers almost continuously through to the cold weather. The stems, being flexible, are easy to fan out against a wall or fence.

Amadeus

HEIGHT *2.5m (8ft)* SPREAD *1m (3ft)*
FLOWERING *Repeat* TYPE *Climber*
SCENT *Light* CULTIVAR *'Korlabriax'*

It is difficult to breed healthy roses with big red flowers, but those of 'Amadeus' are an unfading, rain-resistant, bright crimson, and up to 10cm (4in) across. It is healthy and winter hardy, and has won a number of awards around the world. Its medium vigour makes it particularly suitable for growing against a wall or fence where space is limited. Also an excellent choice for an obelisk or pillar.

Bathsheba

HEIGHT *3m (10ft)* SPREAD *2m (6ft)*
FLOWERING *Repeat*
TYPE *Climbing English rose*
SCENT *Strong myrrh*
CULTIVAR *'Auschimbley'*

This rose makes a strong impression in the garden. It is the perfect size for a wall or fence, where it can be easily kept under control, and its flowers can be easily accessed for regular smelling and cutting. The flowers are 10cm (4in) or more across and have about 170 beautifully arranged petals. Their fragrance is superb, a delicious floral myrrh with hints of tea and honey. They are a beautiful blend of subtle apricot-pink and soft yellow, paling to cream on the outer petals. A healthy rose that repeat-flowers well.

Lady of Shalott

HEIGHT *3m (10ft)* SPREAD *2m (6ft)*
FLOWERING *Repeat*
TYPE *English rose* SCENT *Medium to strong tea and fruit*
CULTIVAR *'Ausnyson'*

A versatile and beautiful rose, one of the best of the English roses. It is normally grown as a substantial shrub (p.97), but it will quickly cover a 2–3m (6–10ft) high wall or fence, especially in warmer climates. The flowers are produced almost continuously from late spring/early summer until late in the year and, given a good spell of weather, a few flowers will open up in winter which are ideal for bringing into the house. The unopened buds are a rich orange-red opening to apricot. They have a delicious fragrance, a soft tea with hints of spiced apple and cloves. A very healthy rose.

Wollerton Old Hall

HEIGHT *3m (10ft)*
SPREAD *2m (6ft)*
FLOWERING *Repeat*
TYPE *Climbing English rose*
SCENT *Strong myrrh*
CULTIVAR *'Ausblanket'*

'Wollerton Old Hall' is remarkable for the strength of its fragrance and the size of its flowers. It is a healthy, fairly vigorous variety and so needs a good-sized wall or fence to grow on, although the stems aren't too stiff, so it can be fanned out quite easily. The unopened buds have flashes of red on the outside, the flowers opening to the softest pale apricot before paling a little with age. They are beautifully rounded, the central stamens rarely showing themselves, although still easily accessible to bees. The fragrance is a particularly strong, warm myrrh with hints of citrus, although some say magnolia.

'Guirlande d'Amour'

Guirlande d'Amour

HEIGHT *2.5m (8ft)* SPREAD *2m (6ft)*
FLOWERING *Repeat* TYPE *Climbing hybrid musk*
SCENT *Strong* CULTIVAR *'Lenalbi'*

'Guirlande d'Amour' produces a mass of pure white flowers in huge pyramids of up to 80 blooms. Its flowers are semi-double, with stamens in full view, giving off a strong, musky, clove fragrance, typical of this group of roses. It can also be grown as a beautiful, arching shrub. A healthy and reliable rose.

Sourire d'Isabelle

HEIGHT *2.5m (8ft)* SPREAD *2m (6ft)*
FLOWERING *Repeat* TYPE *Climbing hybrid musk*
SCENT *Light* CULTIVAR *'Vel10kgual'*

A healthy and easy-to-control climber. Its flowers are single, soft pink on the outside paling to white in the middle. They are produced freely on a plant that can be grown as either a climber or an arching shrub, depending on how it is pruned. The stamens are a showy purple-orange, ageing to purple-pink. If not dead-headed, 'Sourire d'Isabelle' produces a good crop of orange hips.

'Sourire d'Isabelle'

Roses for growing through trees

It is the natural habit of many wild roses to scramble up trees – that is what their thorns are for. A rambler tumbling through a big tree is a magnificent sight, and smaller trees can also look charming with more compact roses through them.

'Kew Rambler'

Kew Rambler

HEIGHT *5m (16ft)* SPREAD *3m (10ft)* FLOWERING *Once*
TYPE *Rambler* SCENT *Strong musk*

One of the parents of 'Kew Rambler' is *Rosa soulieana*, a rarely seen climbing species with small creamy flowers, grey foliage, and many thorns. 'Kew Rambler' has inherited the last two characteristics, but its flowers are bigger and quite a bright pink with a white eye. In autumn there is a good crop of small orange hips.

Francis E. Lester

HEIGHT *5m (16ft)* SPREAD *3m (10ft)* FLOWERING *Once*
TYPE *Rambler* SCENT *Strong musk*

This is a wonderfully free-flowering rambler, the small single flowers being produced in large heads. They are a gentle, soft pink, paling to white in the centre, the whole flower eventually turning that colour. The petals drop cleanly (important in a rambler when the great majority of blooms will be out of reach) and are followed by an abundance of small orange-red hips that last well into the winter until the birds feast on them. The fragrance is the classic musk type found in ramblers, which wafts on the wind, making it perceptible from some distance away. 'Francis E. Lester' can also be trained on pergolas where its flowers will be more in reach. Altogether a healthy, tough, beautiful, and garden-worthy rose.

Rosa filipes 'Kiftsgate'

HEIGHT *12m (40ft) or more* SPREAD *8m (26ft) or more*
FLOWERING *Once* TYPE *Rambling species rose*
SCENT *Strong musk*

Not a rose for the fainthearted, this is the most vigorous of all varieties. The one growing at Kiftsgate Court (after which it was named) is at least 25m (80ft) tall, growing up a copper beech tree. If space can be found, it is distinctive and beautiful. It has pale bronze-green young leaves. The individual flowers are white, quite small but borne in huge, airy clusters of 100 or more, and emit a delicious musk fragrance. They are followed by beautiful and long-lasting small rose-red hips. It can be grown in other situations, but will send out 3-4m (10–13ft) shoots each year and needs a lot of management.

'Francis E. Lester'

Rosa filipes 'Kiftsgate'

Adélaïde d'Orléans

HEIGHT *5m (16ft)* SPREAD *3m (10ft)* FLOWERING *Once*
TYPE *Rambler* SCENT *Light to medium musk*

With its very lax growth, 'Adélaïde d'Orléans' is a
superb choice for growing into a tree. The festoons of
semi-double flowers hang down gracefully, and they
look good contrasted against a dark-leaved tree such as
a conifer or copper beech. 'Adélaïde d'Orléans' is not
excessively vigorous, and would take a few years to
overwhelm, say, a mature apple tree. It is a shame that it
doesn't produce hips or have a strong fragrance, but its
beautiful flowers make up for those shortfalls. It is a
very healthy rose and more or less evergreen, at least in
the UK.

American Pillar

HEIGHT *5m (16ft)* SPREAD *3m (10ft)* FLOWERING *Once*
TYPE *Rambler* SCENT *Light*

A rather brightly coloured, vigorous rambler that is
completely reliable and good for adding a splash of
colour to a garden. The flowers are held in large clusters,
and are an intense pink with a strongly contrasting
white base. In the autumn the leaves colour up and
bright red hips are produced. It is very winter hardy.

Climbing Cécile Brunner

HEIGHT *8m (26ft)* SPREAD *4m (13ft)*
FLOWERING *Once* TYPE *Climber* SCENT *Medium sweet*

A mature plant of the climbing form of 'Cécile Brunner'
in full flower is a sight not easily forgotten. The
abundance of flowers is breathtaking, each bud like a
miniature hybrid tea with scrolled petals. As the buds
open up they form a rosette shape with a button eye and
the colour fades from clear pink to blush. It is essentially
a once-flowering rose, but a few later flowers are
produced. This climbing form originated from the
original 'Cécile Brunner', which is only about 1m (3ft)
tall and repeat-flowers very well – otherwise it
is identical.

Rambling Rector

HEIGHT *8m (26ft)* SPREAD *5m (16ft)*
FLOWERING *Once* TYPE *Rambler* SCENT *Strong musk*

A vigorous rose, 'Rambling Rector' is better suited to
growing through trees than to being trained against a
wall, where it will soon become a difficult-to-manage
monster. It will grow up through the branches, hanging
on by its many thorns, and producing long, strongly
fragrant festoons of small semi-double, pure-white
flowers. These are soon followed by small orange hips
that last into the winter and are eventually taken by the
birds. 'Rambling Rector' needs a large tree such as an
oak, beech, or ash (it can easily swallow up and kill
smaller ones). Rather surprisingly, it can also be grown
as a large weeping standard, although this needs plenty
of space and stout staking.

'Adélaïde d'Orléans'

'Climbing Cécile Brunner'

'American Pillar'

'Rambling Rector'

Blush Rambler

HEIGHT *4m (13ft)* SPREAD *3m (10ft)*
FLOWERING *Once* TYPE *Rambler* SCENT *Strong musk*

A reliable and valuable rambler. The flowers are soft pink overall (although there is a fair bit of variation) and there aren't many roses in that shade that are also tough, healthy, and not too vigorous. The petals drop cleanly once each flower has finished – important in a tall rambler. It also has a delicious musk fragrance and few thorns. Lovely in a medium-sized tree but not so vigorous that it is too big for a pergola.

Rosa banksiae 'Lutea'

HEIGHT *7m (23ft)* SPREAD *3m (10ft)* FLOWERING *Once*
TYPE *Rambling species rose* SCENT *Light*

If, in spring, you spot a vigorous climber with an abundance of small bright-yellow flowers, it is likely to be *Rosa banksiae* 'Lutea', also known as Lady Banks' rose. It is extremely free-flowering and the colour is a delight to the eye at that time of year. It is best suited to a Mediterranean climate; in the UK it can get cut back if there is a really hard frost, although it still performs well. It has no thorns at all, and so apparently nothing to keep it attached to a tree, but it will still successfully scramble through them, and is easier to manage like this than on most walls. The single white form, *R. banksiae* var. *normalis*, has the most wonderful violet fragrance; unfortunately only faint in 'Lutea'.

Rosa banksiae 'Lutea'

'Blush Rambler'

'Treasure Trove'

Treasure Trove

HEIGHT *10m (33ft)*   SPREAD *5m (16ft)*
FLOWERING *Once*   TYPE *Rambler*   SCENT *Medium sweet*

The original seedling of this was found in the garden of Mr John Treasure below a 'Kiftsgate' rose and near a 'Buff Beauty', and so it is supposed that they are the two parents. It certainly has the extreme vigour of 'Kiftsgate' and the medium-sized apricot flowers are reminiscent of 'Buff Beauty'. They fade with age and sometimes become quite pink in the heat. The young leaves are particularly richly coloured and a lovely feature, as are the medium-sized, rounded red hips that last well into late winter. There is no variety with the same vigour that is similar in appearance.

ROSE
care

Giving your roses the best start

The two fundamentals for healthy, free-flowering roses in
the garden are to choose a variety that is tough, reliable,
and disease-resistant, and then to prepare the ground
well and plant it well. For the first, take a look at the
Rose Selector (pp.86–203); for the second, read on.

Bare-root or container-grown?

Having selected a variety, you have the option of buying it either dormant
with no soil attached (known as "bare root"), or as an actively growing,
often flowering plant in a container. So, which should you choose?

There is a much wider range of varieties available as bare-root plants via
mail order from nurseries, but they are only available from early winter
through to mid-spring. They are dug from the field and are cheap, easy, and
environmentally friendly to dispatch, making a small, light parcel. Since
they have no leaves they suffer little or no stress from being transplanted,
although it's crucial the roots are not allowed to dry out at any time between
receipt and planting. If you can't plant the rose straight away, perhaps
because it's frosty or too wet, it's best to quickly "heel it in" – dig a hole just
large enough to bury the roots and the bottom 5cm (2in) of the stem,
firming the soil back around them. The rose should be happy like this for
several weeks if necessary.

Containerized roses are available year round both from garden centres
and via mail order. They require a plastic pot, potting compost, and several
months of watering and general care before they are ready for sale, and
delivery involves large boxes and couriers. If you're buying in person, check
the plant looks healthy and well cared for. A containerized rose in flower
will make an immediate effect in your garden, but it will need extra care and
attention to thrive after the stress of being transplanted.

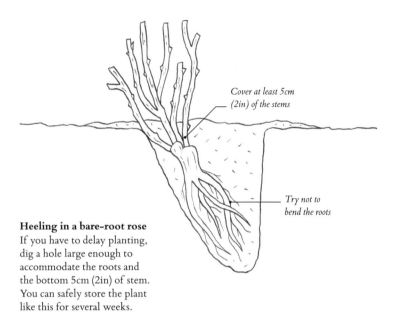

Cover at least 5cm
(2in) of the stems

Try not to
bend the roots

Heeling in a bare-root rose
If you have to delay planting,
dig a hole large enough to
accommodate the roots and
the bottom 5cm (2in) of stem.
You can safely store the plant
like this for several weeks.

Getting the position right

As long as good, tough varieties are chosen, roses are generally not too
fussy about where they are planted, as long as they get at least five or six
hours of full sun a day during the summer. (There are some exceptions:
shade-tolerant roses, for instance, will manage with only three or four
hours of full sun a day; see pp.176–81.) In hot climates, roses may well
benefit from being shaded from the ravages of the afternoon sun. If the site
is wind-swept, choose varieties that can cope well with this, for example the
Rosa spinosissima and *Rosa rugosa* hybrids.

   Planting at the foot of a wall, especially a south- or east-facing wall
that's sheltered from the prevailing wind and rain, offers an extra challenge,
since the soil is likely to be very dry. There needs to be at least 50cm (18in)
depth of good soil, which doesn't sit on solid rock or foundations. Make the
planting hole as big as you can, and incorporate extra organic matter into

the soil to retain moisture. If the site is underneath the overhang of a roof, you'll need to plant a short distance away from the wall, where the rain will reach the rose. An occasional deep soaking and the generous use of an annual mulch will help to conserve moisture, although it is important to do this before the rose shows signs of stress.

Excessive competition at the roots from trees and hedges can be a problem, especially while roses are getting established. If there are a lot of roots, it's best to plant further away or to cut the other plant's roots back to give the rose's roots extra growing space. Ramblers and species roses generally cope better, and will grow well despite being planted at the foot of trees, although they may need a year or two to get established.

Make sure there's enough room for your chosen rose. Use the height and spread information given in pp.86–203 as a guide for planting distances. If you're planting a hedge, plant them half their width apart.

Preparing the ground

Roses need a moisture-retentive soil that never becomes water-logged. Provided that the soil is neither heavy clay nor free-draining and sandy, it should be suitable for rose-growing. That being said, all soils can be improved by incorporating well-rotted organic matter when you plant, and mulching regularly from then on. This will help with moisture retention, and will feed all the myriad organisms that are so important to the health of the soil and the plants growing in it. The pH (acidity/alkalinity) of the soil should ideally be around neutral (pH 7), although anything between 6 and 7.5 will be fine. It is worthwhile spending time and, if necessary, money on trying to ensure the soil is as suitable as possible for the rose *before* planting. Once planted, improving the soil at root level is very difficult.

The organic matter can be in the form of home-made compost or animal manure, but both must be well rotted, otherwise the rotting process will use up nitrogen and so starve the rose. Buying some soil improver – generally a blend of animal manure and plant waste, which should be well rotted and free of both viable weed seeds and living weeds – may be easiest. Home-made compost and manures are often full of weed material and can create a lot of extra work. Whatever organic matter one uses it shouldn't be added to excess – one or two spadefuls per planting hole, mixed in with the excavated soil, is adequate as long as the soil is reasonably good. Poorer soils benefit from a bit more, but don't add more than about a quarter extra: it's liable to rot down and disappear, causing the soil level to dip and the soil to shrink away from the roots. Species roses and other once-flowering types will often be fine with little or no improvement to the soil.

Replacing a rose

If you want to plant where a rose has been growing, you'll need to do some extra preparation to avoid the risk of replant disease, whose symptoms are poor growth and slow establishment of the new rose. Often this is simply due to the soil being worn out – perhaps it hasn't been mulched for years, or is compacted and devoid of the soil-borne organisms that are vital for strong growth. If the soil where the previous rose was growing looks in good heart – easy to dig, with plenty of worms and other creatures in it – then you can just prepare and plant as normal, and the new rose will grow away, especially if you apply mycorrhizal fungi at planting time.

If you suspect the soil is worn out, the fastest option, if you only want to plant a few roses, is to change the soil for each plant in a hole 50 x 50cm (18 x 18in) square and just as deep. It is important to be very fussy about the replacement soil – bought-in soil is often free-draining, has little or no organic matter, a high pH, and lacks structure – all characteristics that roses do not like. For one or two roses this is not too much work, but for a bed with, say, 20 it is a more serious undertaking. The alternative is to add generous quantities of well-rotted organic matter and grow a cover crop like the pretty, blue-flowered *Phacelia tanacetifolia* for two or three years before planting the new roses. This needs to be sown direct into the soil in spring and dug in once it's finished flowering.

Preparing and planting the rose

The roots of bare-root roses should never be allowed to dry out. They should be kept in their original packaging in a cool, frost-free place, or heeled in if necessary (pp.206–207). Take them out an hour or two before you want to plant them and plunge them in a bucket of water until you have a hole ready to plant them in.

The compost of container-grown roses is often dry and difficult to re-wet once the rose is in the ground. If you plant it like this, the rose is likely to suffer from stress, take longer to get established, and be more vulnerable to pests and diseases. It is crucial therefore to soak it thoroughly by submerging the whole container in water for an hour or so before you're ready to plant, and then allowing it to drain. If, when you remove it from the pot, the roots form a solid mass and are circling around (that is, the rose was rootbound), they should be broken up and disentangled to encourage them to spread into the surrounding soil.

The hole you dig should be wide enough to accommodate the roots without bending them over and deep enough that the bud union – the point of attachment of the green shoots to the brown roots – is about 5cm (2in) below ground.

While the roots are wet, it's a good idea to sprinkle powdered mycorrhizal fungi on them. These fungi help plants extract water and nutrients from the soil, and there is evidence they can help roses to establish, and to grow better in poor soils. The only time they can be applied is when planting, since they need to be in direct contact with the roots. It's a good idea to hold the rose over the planting hole while sprinkling them, so that any excess that doesn't stick to the roots is not wasted.

Check the rose is at the right depth in the hole, with the point where the roots attach to the top-growth 5cm (2in) below ground level. Backfill with the soil and organic matter mix and firm in well, although not excessively. Water the newly planted rose, especially if the soil is at all dry. If it was container-grown it will definitely need generous watering straight after planting, and also for the next few months if it's in full leaf and you plant it in the summer.

Transplanting

Roses can be transplanted successfully even if several years old. Small varieties are the easiest to move: they should be fine at ten years old, but a big rambler with extensive roots would be a real struggle to re-establish after as little as five years. Dig the rose up in winter and plant it immediately – dig the hole first! If there's any delay at all, keep the roots moist in a bucket of water or else heel the rose in until you can plant it properly.

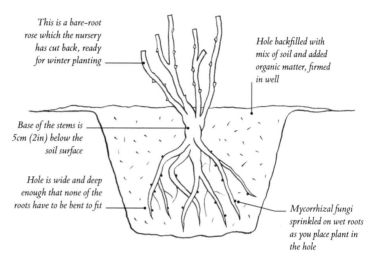

This is a bare-root rose which the nursery has cut back, ready for winter planting

Hole backfilled with mix of soil and added organic matter, firmed in well

Base of the stems is 5cm (2in) below the soil surface

Hole is wide and deep enough that none of the roots have to be bent to fit

Mycorrhizal fungi sprinkled on wet roots as you place plant in the hole

Planting a rose
Soak both bare-root and container-grown roses for an hour or so before you plant them, and water well immediately afterwards.

Care in the first year

Bare-root roses will not need much extra watering in the first year unless the soil becomes very dry. Container-grown roses, though, will need regular watering. Make a low wall of soil, about 60cm (2ft) in diameter, around each rose to prevent the water escaping.

Make sure you maintain a clear space around each rose, especially for the first year or two. Ideally, mulch 50–75cm (18–24in) around it to help retain moisture and feed the soil, and keep that area free of weeds and encroaching plants.

Growing roses in containers

For most shrub roses, the container needs to be at least 50cm (18in) in diameter and the same in depth. Climbers need more space – at least 60cm (2ft) wide and deep. The bigger the container, the greater the availability of water and nutrients, thus reducing the risk of the rose running out of either.

You can fill your pot with a good-quality peat-free potting compost, or home-made garden compost that's completely rotted and free of perennial weeds, mixed 50:50 with good-quality soil. The soil will help with long-term nutrient supply and will retain water, while the compost will help to aerate the mix. The soil also adds weight, which will help to prevent the pot blowing over, especially if it's plastic. It's a good idea to raise the container up on pot feet, to ensure it doesn't sit in water in wet weather.

Roses growing in pots need regular and generous watering. It is important to assess the moisture levels in the pot by digging down 15cm (6in) or so. The potting mix often contracts when dry, so that the water runs down the sides of it and straight out the bottom of the pot. If this happens, a spell of frequent watering will be necessary to re-wet it.

Propagating roses

In order to produce roses in bulk, commercial growers propagate roses by budding or grafting, where a single vegetative bud of the variety is carefully inserted under the bark of a rootstock and covered up. In midwinter, once it has knitted in place, the rootstock above the bud is cut off, which stimulates the growth of the grafted bud.

Since this process is a skilled operation and requires a suitable rootstock, grafting is best left to the experts. Home gardeners can instead propagate their roses by taking cuttings. This technique works for most varieties, although some roses are rather reluctant and others will refuse altogether.

The best time to take cuttings is from summer through to the autumn, when it should be easy to find a stem that is semi-ripe and still has some flexibility, and has flowered recently. The cutting should be about 15–20cm (6–8in) long. Since roots can emerge from anywhere along the stem, it doesn't matter how close to a bud you cut. Remove the growing tip, including any soft growth beneath it and all but two or three upper leaves. Insert each cutting to half its length, either into the ground in a sheltered position, or in a pot filled with peat-free seed and cutting compost in a shady spot in a greenhouse or cold frame. Water the cuttings well, and continue to keep the compost moist. Once your cuttings are growing strongly and have a good root system – which can take from a few weeks to a year, depending on how warm it is – they can be moved to a more open nursery bed or potted on. Don't be tempted to try and move them too soon: the young roots are very delicate.

An alternative propagation method, suitable for varieties whose stems can be easily bent down to the ground (such as ramblers and ground-cover roses), is known as layering. This simply means cutting partway through a stem, burying it a little, and pegging it in place. After a year or so, roots should have formed, and the rooted stem can be cut from the parent plant and transplanted.

Seed collected from garden-grown roses will turn out different to its parent plant, due to insects cross-pollinating varieties. Unfortunately, the results are nearly always much worse, but it can be fun to grow the seed and see what results. It should be taken from ripe hips and kept in a plastic bag in a fridge for two months before sowing. Once sown, keep in a warm, light place but below 15°C (60°F), since higher temperatures can inhibit germination. This is how new varieties are created, although many tens of thousands of seeds are usually required to find a single garden-worthy rose.

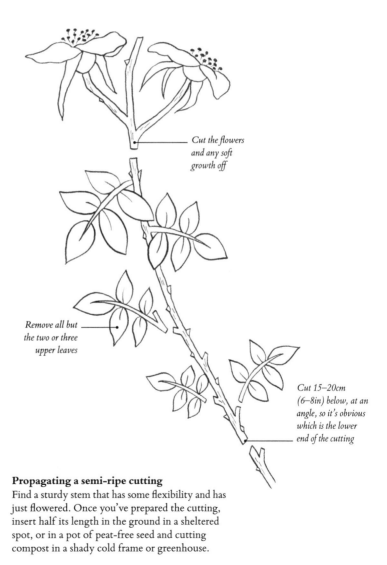

Cut the flowers and any soft growth off

Remove all but the two or three upper leaves

Cut 15–20cm (6–8in) below, at an angle, so it's obvious which is the lower end of the cutting

Propagating a semi-ripe cutting
Find a sturdy stem that has some flexibility and has just flowered. Once you've prepared the cutting, insert half its length in the ground in a sheltered spot, or in a pot of peat-free seed and cutting compost in a shady cold frame or greenhouse.

Looking after your roses

Once established, species roses and their hybrids can be left to their own devices, but most other types will benefit from a little more regular care.

Weeding & mulching

It's important for the health of your roses to keep the area immediately around them free of competition, so check regularly for any encroaching plants, whether weeds or vigorous neighbours outgrowing their space, and remove them. This will also ensure good air flow, which helps to reduce fungal infections.

To grow well, roses (and indeed all plants) need the soil to be in good condition. The best way to keep it that way is by regular mulching. A thick layer of mulch protects the soil from the elements, buries diseased leaves, helps with moisture retention and weed control, and prevents compaction. Most importantly, it encourages the proliferation of the myriad organisms that keep the soil healthy.

Mulch is simply a layer of organic matter that is applied to the top of the soil. It doesn't need to be particularly well rotted since it stays on the surface. As long as it's free of weeds, it can consist of bark or wood chips, manure, garden compost, old potting compost, or spent mushroom compost (only if the soil is below pH 7, as it is quite alkaline). The material shouldn't be too fine or it may create a waterproof barrier.

The best time to apply a mulch is soon after pruning (pp.217–22), as there will be room to get in between the plants without knocking off young shoots. Spread the material in a layer 5–10cm (2–4in) thick, and if necessary top up any thin areas through the year.

Watering

While roses will survive long periods of drought, to grow well and produce plenty of long-lasting flowers they need moisture at their roots. The amount of watering you'll need to do will depend on the weather and how free-draining your soil is. The best way to assess moisture levels is to dig a little hole about 15–20cm (6–8in) deep from time to time. If the base feels dry or not particularly moist, give them a good soaking. It is always better to water occasionally but thoroughly, to encourage deep roots. While an automatic drip-irrigation system can be helpful, it needs careful monitoring to check that it's not either making the soil waterlogged or only damping the surface of the soil.

It's important to avoid splashing water on leaves, as this encourages many diseases. If you use a sprinkler system, or can't avoid wetting the leaves with your hose, it's best to water your roses a little before the warmest point of the day, as this will help the leaves to dry out quickly. Early morning or evening watering, conversely, will result in leaves staying wet for a number of hours, increasing the chance of disease.

Feeding

While feeding roses is not essential, most varieties will benefit – especially those that have a long flowering period, which can drain the plants of energy. Any granular fertilizer with a nitrogen:phosphorus:potassium (NPK) ratio of around 5:5:10 will work well – the extra potassium supports flower production. Avoid those with a higher proportion of nitrogen (N), since they'll encourage lots of soft growth that will be less able to hold up a crop of flowers, while being more susceptible to pests and diseases.

The first feed should coincide with the start of strong spring growth, with a second one at the time of the first flush of flowers. A third application may be helpful in late summer, although no later as it can encourage soft young growth at a time when it will be more susceptible to frost damage. Never apply more than the recommended amount, since this can do more harm than good. Scatter the granules around evenly in the area under the bush and water them in well if no rain is forecast.

Spraying or watering the leaves with a foliar feed may make them more resistant to disease. Seaweed-based ones seem to be particularly effective; as are those made with comfrey or nettles (though they're incredibly smelly).

Species roses and their near hybrids will usually not need any feeding, and once-flowering roses should be fine with just one application in spring.

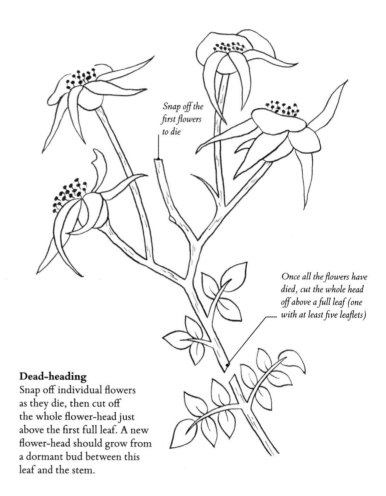

Snap off the first flowers to die

Once all the flowers have died, cut the whole head off above a full leaf (one with at least five leaflets)

Dead-heading
Snap off individual flowers as they die, then cut off the whole flower-head just above the first full leaf. A new flower-head should grow from a dormant bud between this leaf and the stem.

Dead-heading

Regularly removing spent flowers keeps the rose looking good and encourages more flowers. This is particularly important if the petals don't drop off cleanly, leaving the rose covered with decaying flowers. Each bloom can be removed as it dies simply by snapping it off. Once all blooms on a head are spent, cut it back to the first full leaf (one that has five or seven leaflets) with secateurs. Don't dead-head too late in the season, as this can encourage soft new growth that will be more susceptible to frost damage.

Once-flowering varieties don't need dead-heading unless they look unattractive. Roses grown for their hips, whether once- or repeat-flowering, shouldn't be dead-headed. If you're reluctant to lose the later flowers, you could experiment with only removing half the heads; or try dead-heading until late summer, and see if the hips still ripen in the remaining time.

Pruning and training

Much has been written about how to prune roses, with many supposedly important rules and regulations about what one should or shouldn't do. All this has made what is a relatively simple task into a seemingly very complicated one.

Many of the rules and regulations are left over from the time when roses were grown for exhibition purposes. They are for gardeners who were trying to grow the perfect bloom for the show bench, using varieties that bear little resemblance to the great majority of roses we grow today.

You prune a rose in order to create an attractively shaped plant that will flower as much, and as beautifully, as possible. Pruning can also keep the rose within the space you want it to fill, and help limit pests and diseases that overwinter on leaves and some older stems. Thinning out the main stems encourages good air flow and stimulates healthy new growth.

Pruning different types of roses

Given the wide variety of shapes and growth habits in roses, it's no surprise that each type is best suited to a particular pruning method. That said, it's worth remembering that supposedly bad pruning will never do any permanent damage to the rose. You'll build your confidence from year to year by trial-and-error and observation.

Repeat-flowering shrub roses, along with climbers and ramblers, are perhaps the most common rose types grown by home gardeners; as such, I've offered more detailed pruning tips for them on pp.218–20. For other varieties, read on.

Species roses and their hybrids

These shouldn't be pruned at all. They've grown happily, unpruned, for millions of years; pruning would spoil their shape and reduce the number of flowers and hips they produce. At most, you may need to remove the odd big woody stem at the base after a decade or two of growth, to rejuvenate the plant.

Once-flowering and tea roses

Although these can be pruned the same way as repeat-flowering shrub roses, there is a good argument for treating the once-flowering roses (essentially the gallicas, damasks, albas, centifolias, and mosses) slightly differently. These old roses have a different character to the repeat-flowerers, which can easily be lost if they are over-pruned. A light pruning, reducing their height by perhaps a quarter and leaving some wayward stems, will help to retain that character. Cut out any diseased or rubbing stems, but don't be tempted to thin or tidy them up too much.

Tea roses can flower more or less continuously, and resent being pruned too much. Once the bush is a few years old, simply cut out one or two of the least-productive stems each year to encourage fresh new growth from the base.

Hybrid teas and floribundas

These may need pruning a little harder than other shrub roses (see below) to help maintain their shape and prevent them growing lanky. If you want them to produce bigger flowers on stronger stems (like those exhibited in flower shows), you can prune them much harder, but this will weaken the plants and shorten their life-span.

Standard roses

These should be pruned rather harder than you would the same variety grown without the long stem, since if the top is allowed to get too big it will be top-heavy and likely to break or be blown over. Shape it to encourage a spherical head.

Repeat-flowering shrub roses

At its simplest, pruning shrub roses (that is, all roses that aren't species roses, climbers, or ramblers) can just mean reducing the height of the rose by about half, depending on how tall you want the rose to be in that position. A hard prune will result in a shorter plant, while a lighter one will produce a taller rose. For better results, however, it is worth understanding how a rose grows and flowers before you prune.

Look at the rose: you'll notice that flowers are produced from side shoots growing from the main stems. These need to pruned back to about 10–15cm (4–6in), around the time that new growth is starting (pp.220–221). This encourages the plant to produce more side shoots, which will flower the same season. Cut any non-flowering stems down to about the same height as the other stems you have just cut.

Also look for any stems that look old – rough and brown in contrast to the smooth, young green stems. Cut these out: they will probably produce poor-quality flowers, and if you trace them to the top they will often show weak growth. They are also more likely to suffer from disease. Finally, remove any dead, diseased, or particularly weak-looking stems, along with any remaining leaves.

If all of the stems look very old, rejuvenative pruning may be the best option (p.221).

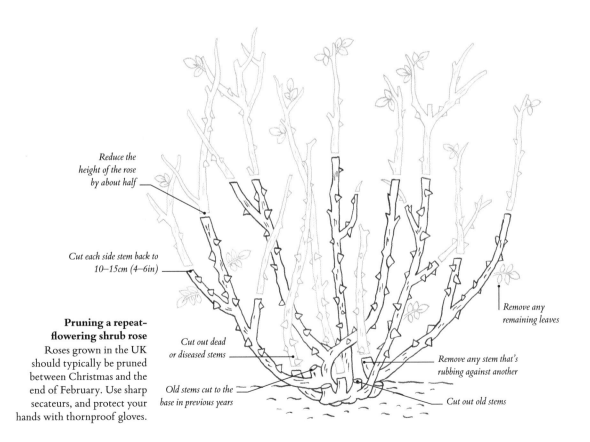

Reduce the height of the rose by about half

Cut each side stem back to 10–15cm (4–6in)

Remove any remaining leaves

Cut out dead or diseased stems

Remove any stem that's rubbing against another

Old stems cut to the base in previous years

Cut out old stems

Pruning a repeat-flowering shrub rose
Roses grown in the UK should typically be pruned between Christmas and the end of February. Use sharp secateurs, and protect your hands with thornproof gloves.

Having finished, step back and assess the plant. Does it look balanced? Is it the shape and size you want? Have all the dead or diseased stems been removed? Make any further tweaks and then remove any leaves remaining on the stems, since they are likely to carry over pests and disease from one season to the next. It's also good to weed around the rose and then mulch the ground beneath it to bury any fallen leaves, which may harbour pests or diseases.

Climbers and ramblers

Far more important than the process of pruning, when it comes to climbers and ramblers, is choosing the right variety in the first place. Try and match the vigour of the rose with the size of the structure or area that you want it to cover. Do not be tempted to choose a variety that will reach the top of the wall or obelisk in one or two seasons, since it will simply carry on growing and become a menace.

Any climber or rambler you want to train against a structure such as a fence or an arch (p.222) can be pruned in the same way. In terms of flowering, climbers and ramblers work in a similar way to repeat-flowering shrubs, the only difference being that the flowering side shoots are produced off much longer main stems. Let these main stems grow as long as you need them to be, and shorten the side shoots to about 5–15cm (2–6in), depending on how neat a look is required. If you want to keep the growth tight, reduce them to one or two buds, or around 5cm (2in). Leave them longer for a more informal look. As with shrub roses, once they've been pruned, the side shoots will produce more side shoots which should be pruned in the same way the following winter. This process can carry on until the original stem starts looking old and tired, at which stage it should be cut out completely.

When growing up trees, ramblers are effectively inaccessible for pruning and have to be left alone. They will cope perfectly well without any help from secateurs.

Making the cuts

The general rule, for whatever climate you live in, is to prune roses when new growth is just starting. Any earlier and there is a risk of prematurely encouraging young shoots that will then be susceptible to frost damage. Any later and many young shoots will be lost by cutting or knocking them off, since the roses will be actively growing by then; the first flowers will therefore appear later.

In the UK and other countries with a similar climate, sometime between Christmas and the end of February is ideal. In Mediterranean climates with little frost, pruning can start in late November or early December, but should finish by the end of January. In hot climates, the period of dormancy may well be in midsummer and so the main prune should be done then.

If a rose sends out long shoots towards the end of the year, it's good to cut these back by a third to a half to prevent them breaking in winter winds and to keep the plant looking reasonably tidy.

The only tool you'll need for nearly all pruning tasks is a good pair of sharp secateurs. If the rose is old with substantial stems, you'll also need loppers and a pruning saw. Gloves are pretty essential – not so thin that the thorns puncture them but not so thick that they limit your movement.

Most "rules" about how and where a rose stem should be pruned can be safely ignored. While some will tell you that the stem must be cut at an angle, in fact this makes no difference. This rule may well have come from the days before secateurs were invented, when pruning was done with a knife and involved slicing at an angle. Indeed, it is probably better to cut straight across, since it exposes less cut stem. The distance above the bud is not crucial either. While there may be some dieback if a cut is made a few centimetres above a bud, it is rarely of any consequence and is soon hidden by leaves. And life is too short to worry about searching for that outward-pointing bud! Better to concentrate on cutting the stem at the right place to create an attractively shaped plant.

Rejuvenating a neglected rose

If a rose hasn't been pruned properly (or, indeed, at all) for a number of years, the stems will have become old and woody and the rose too tall. The simplest way of dealing with this is to cut all the stems hard back to around 30cm (1ft). This can either be done all in one season or, if the rose is looking a bit feeble, stretched out over two. With a bit of luck new shoots will be produced in spring, seemingly from nowhere, and a beautifully rejuvenated rose will result.

Training a climbing rose on a structure

The simplest support system is rust-proof screws spaced at regular intervals. You need about 2.5cm (1in) to protrude from the wall, so 7.5cm (3in) screws work well. Trellis is another quick and easy option. Stems should be tied on rather than tucked behind as this may push the trellis away in time and will make cutting older stems out much more difficult. A less conspicuous support is horizontal wires about 50cm (18in) apart, attached to vine eyes to keep them away from the wall. Tensioners should be used to keep the wires taut, and the stems should be tied on to the outside of the wires.

String is the obvious choice for tying the rose stems to their supports, and should be thick and strong enough that it does not break in windy conditions. Tie loosely, to allow for the stems to grow and get thicker. Hollow, stretchy plastic tubing is a good alternative. Wire should not be used as it will easily cut into the stem.

Stems trained horizontally or diagonally will produce more flowers than vertical shoots, so your aim should be to fan them out to fill the space you have and tie them on to the screws or supporting wires with soft twine.

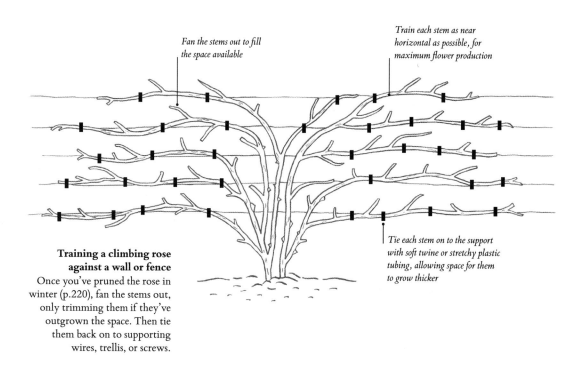

Fan the stems out to fill the space available

Train each stem as near horizontal as possible, for maximum flower production

Tie each stem on to the support with soft twine or stretchy plastic tubing, allowing space for them to grow thicker

Training a climbing rose against a wall or fence
Once you've pruned the rose in winter (p.220), fan the stems out, only trimming them if they've outgrown the space. Then tie them back on to supporting wires, trellis, or screws.

If your rose isn't thriving

Any problem is easiest to remedy if spotted early, but most can be put right – in the most drastic cases, by removing it altogether.

Prevention is better than cure

The easiest ways to ensure a rose stays healthy is to choose a naturally disease-resistant variety in the first place, and to prepare the ground well before planting (pp.208–209). It's also a good idea to mix roses with other plants. This makes it more difficult for pests and diseases to move from one rose to the next, and encourages beneficial insects that will help reduce pest numbers. Give each rose enough space to ensure good airflow, so that the leaves dry quickly, thereby reducing the incidence of disease. Good pruning, regular mulching, feeding, and watering (if necessary) will also keep your roses in top health.

The lower the level of disease in your garden, the healthier your roses are likely to stay, as there'll be fewer disease spores floating around. If, despite your best efforts, the rose becomes badly diseased and its condition does not improve, replace it with a more naturally disease-resistant one. Make sure to improve the soil first if planning to replant in the same spot (p.209).

Pests and diseases can easily overwinter on roses. The older the stem, the more likely it is to harbour pests and diseases, which is why old stems should be cut out and fresh new ones allowed to replace them when you prune the rose in winter. Stripping off any remaining leaves and burying any fallen ones under a good layer of mulch will also reduce the chance of reinfection in spring. The harder you prune, the more likely you are to remove all sources of infection, although this should be balanced against the risk of overpruning, which may shorten the rose's life.

Spotting symptoms

Keeping a close eye on your roses and diagnosing any problems early on will ensure that any treatments are much more likely to be effective.

The rose's growth is weak

Sometimes a plant just looks poorly: it may be growing slowly, not producing many flowering stems, or not flowering as much as it should.

• **Is it having to compete with other plants?** A mat of plants growing right round the base of the rose is likely to starve it of water and nutrients. Pull them out and keep the space clear under a mulch of organic material. A tree or hedge close by may also be taking advantage of the extra water and nutrients you're giving the rose. Box and yew hedges are especially guilty of this, since their roots tend to be near the surface. These can be cut back or prevented from encroaching by sinking a thick sheet of polythene to a depth of about 30cm (1ft).

• **Is it getting enough sun?** Most roses need at least six hours of full sun a day in the growing season, and even the more shade-tolerant varieties (pp.176–81) need four hours. If nearby plants are shading the rose out, cut them back; otherwise, the only option is to transplant the rose in winter to a better spot (p.210).

• **Perhaps the soil is too acid or alkaline?** Roses like it to be just either side of neutral, around pH 6–7.5, and don't appreciate anything too much outside of this range. Soil pH can be easily tested using a home kit, and if it's too acid, you can add lime to remedy the problem. Making an alkaline soil more acid is more difficult, but it can be done by using sulphur chips.

• **Is the soil it's planted in getting waterlogged or, at the other extreme, draining too fast?** While roses can cope with a wide range of soil types, they do not like extremes of clay or sand. Both can be improved by using generous quantities of well-rotted organic matter, but this needs to be applied before planting. The only option, therefore, is transplanting (p.210). For similar spots where you'd like to plant roses, the varieties recommended for wild areas on pp.136–41 are better choices.

• **Was it planted where there another rose was previously growing?** Swapping one rose for another can cause rose replant disease, which stunts growth. If the soil is in a reasonable condition, improve it by applying a generous amount of well-rotted organic matter and mycorrhizal fungi. If the soil is seriously depleted, you may need to replace the soil entirely (p.209).

If there's no obvious cause, poor growth may be due to an excess or deficiency of a nutrient. To check for this, you will need to send a soil sample away to a lab for analysis. The most common problems are an excess or deficiency of potassium and/or phosphorus. Deficiencies are easily remedied by applying an appropriate fertilizer. An excess is often the result of applying too much fertilizer or animal manure. There is no quick cure for this as high levels of these nutrients take many years to reduce, during which time moderate amounts of nitrogen only (preferably organic) should be applied. (Excessive nitrogen produces tall stems with little strength and increased susceptibility to pests and diseases.)

Finally, remember that even roses that have been well cared for have a finite lifespan, which depends on the type of rose and the conditions it is growing in. After 15–20 years, many shrub roses will start losing vigour, and you may want to replace them. Climbers, ramblers, and once-flowering old roses and species roses last longer – sometimes 100 years or more.

It's growing unusual stems

In the UK and much of Europe, nearly all roses are budded on to a rootstock, generally *Rosa laxa* and occasionally *Rosa multiflora*. Elsewhere (particularly North America and Australia), the red climber 'Dr Huey' and the white rambler *Rosa fortuneana* are used. This is done to encourage strong growth and make a plant of saleable size as quickly as possible. Unfortunately, the rootstock occasionally starts growing alongside the grafted rose and these suckers, if not removed promptly, can completely swamp it. The easiest way to identify *R. laxa* and *R. multiflora* stems is to examine the youngest emerging leaves: if they have any hint of red, the stem is not a sucker. If they are pure green and the number of leaflets, and the shape and quantity of thorns, differ from the rest of the rose, it's a sucker. Dig down so you can pull it off or cut it out where it joins the root.

If the sucker flowers, that usually makes matters clear. *R. laxa* and *R. multiflora* have small white or pale-pink single flowers, and *R. fortuneana* has small double white flowers. 'Dr Huey' has bright-red semi-double flowers. However, if the sucker has reached this stage, it's probably too late to safely remove it completely without damaging the rose beyond repair. The best solution would be to replace the whole plant or else to cut the suckers back regularly.

Standard or tree roses can sometimes sprout very straight, upright shoots coming from the stem. These should be removed as soon as they are spotted.

It's being eaten

It can be frustrating to find the foliage of your beloved roses peppered with holes, or the stems colonized by pests. Whether you need to be concerned about such damage will depend on the pest in question, and the severity of their impact.

- **The soft growing tips of new leaves and flowerbuds are smothered in tiny bugs.** These are aphids: usually 3–5mm (⅛–¼in) long and generally green but sometimes pink or black. (Their dead remains are white and frequently confused with white fly.) Probably the most commonly seen pest on roses, aphids suck sap and then excrete honeydew that is sticky and can cause sooty (black) mould on the leaves below. They are able to increase their numbers at a phenomenal rate, but luckily are also a popular source of food for a wide range of insects and birds, so are rarely too much of a problem. As a last resort, severe infestations can be controlled by squashing or knocking them off.

- **A window-like effect** on the leaf is caused by slug worms. They are found on the underside of leaves where they eat the leaf content leaving just the upper surface. The damage they cause is usually minor and should be ignored.

- **Leaves rolled into tight tubes,** inside which may be found a tiny caterpillar, shelter the offspring of the leaf-rolling sawfly. Removing the leaves is likely to cause more harm than good.

- **Leaves skeletonized,** leaving only the main veins, are the work of the rose sawfly caterpillar. These hatch in large numbers, and voraciously feed on the leaves. While the damage can be unsightly, it's usually not a serious probem: remove if you spot them, or leave them as food for beneficial insects and birds.

- **Beautifully excised leaf circles** are the art of the leaf-cutter bee. It takes the leaf portions back to its nest to feed its young. It causes no significant damage to the rose, and the precision of its cutting should be admired.

- **Missing buds, young shoots, or whole leaves** will be the work of rabbits, hares, or deer, who are all very fond of rose-related food. The classic symptom of rabbit and hare damage is the absence of leaflets, with just the leaf stalk remaining, as well as scratchings in the soil and droppings. Deer damage is often more severe and frustrating, as they will take the flower buds. There are sprays that can be applied that will deter these herbivores, but they need to be reapplied on a regular basis and also switched around, since the deer may well get used to the smell. The only permanent prevention is to erect a suitable fence. A possible, much cheaper, alternative is to stretch four or five strands of strong fishing line spaced 30cm (1ft)

Aphids

Slug worm

Leaf-rolling sawfly

Rose sawfly

Leaf-cutter bee

Black spot

Downy mildew

Cercospora

apart: the deer will not see them and will hopefully shy away and look elsewhere for something to eat. You could also try planting *Rosa rugosa* and its hybrids, whose very thorny stems may be unpalatable to these browsers.

There are marks on the leaves or stems

There are a number of diseases that cause these symptoms, and they can be tricky to tell apart.

• **Black or charcoal-grey circular spots** on the upper side of the leaf only, 5–10mm (¼–½in) across with a soft edge, or sometimes lines radiating out of them, are caused by black spot – probably the most common of all rose diseases. If the attack is bad, the spots coalesce and the leaves turn yellow between the spots, before dropping off. In severe attacks, the rose loses all its leaves, which weakens it and looks most unattractive.

Leaves staying wet for long periods encourages black spot, which is why it's important to water roses during the day rather than too early or late. Susceptibility is highly variable – some varieties are completely resistant while others are extremely prone. The great majority will get some, and it can be tolerated if not too severe. Apply a foliar feed (seaweed-based, for instance) as soon as you spot the first sign of black spot. (Even better: apply this regularly from the start of the growing season, especially if you know a rose is susceptible). Make sure you give any more vulnerable roses the best possible growing conditions. Only remove leaves if they're badly affected. Removing those that are still partly green will reduce the plant's ability to photosynthesize and so potentially weaken it. Two or three applications of a suitable fungicide may also help.

• **Dark (often dark purple), irregularly shaped areas** indicate downy mildew. They tend to have a sharp edge and are commonly bounded by the leaf veins, on the upper side of the leaf. This often causes severe leaf drop, which in some very susceptible varieties can occur when the dark areas are hardly noticeable. Spots are sometimes also seen on the stems, when they are quite small and more distinctly purple. Downy mildew is particularly prevalent in times of high humidity and when the leaves are wet for long periods, especially in spring and again in autumn. Again, try to minimize the length of time the leaves are wet by watering during the warmth of the day. Susceptibility varies according to the variety, although miniatures and a number of ramblers are more susceptible.

• **Small, dark spots** up to 5mm (¼in) across, developing into rings with grey centres, are a sign of either *Anthracnose* or *Cercospora* fungi. Neither usually cause too much harm. As with black spot and downy mildew, some varieties of rose are prone to infections, and the likelihood of them occurring is increased by the leaves being wet for prolonged periods.

• **White powdery deposits** on leaves and young stems are caused by powdery mildew, which sometimes also causes distortion of the young leaves. It is very variety-specific, some of the wichurana ramblers like 'Dorothy Perkins' being especially susceptible to it. Dryness at the roots or leaves being wet for long periods make it more likely. Paradoxically, wetting the leaves can help to reduce it: the presence of water prevents the spores from germinating. You must do this around the middle of the day, though, when it's windy and sunny, so they dry out quickly.

• **Small yellow spots** on the upper side of the leaf, corresponding with orange pustules on the underside, are a sign of rust. The orange on the underside turns black later in the season. This can cause severe leaf drop and a general reduction in vigour. Resistance is very variable from variety to variety and since it is difficult to control by cultural methods it is particularly important to choose resistant varieties.

• **Mottled leaves,** with no marks visible underneath, are likely the work of leaf hoppers. These green bugs, around 5mm (¼in) long, often fly or hop off the plant when disturbed. They suck the sap but are rarely serious and can safely be ignored.

However, if tiny, insect-like creatures can be seen on the underside of leaves, with mottling and spotting on the upper side, this indicates red spider mite infection. Almost invisible to the naked eye, the mites suck sap from the underside of leaves, weakening the plant. If left unchecked, they eventually form a web-like covering over the top of the shoot. Red spider mites are sometimes seen in the UK, but are more common in hot, dry climates where they can cause serious damage. Regular sprays of water on the underside of the leaves may help to control them.

• **Leaves turning pale**, known as chlorosis, is a symptom that suggests the rose is suffering from a nutrient deficiency, or soil the pH being too high or low. A lab test (p.225) will pinpoint the cause, most often an excess or deficiency of potassium, phosphorus, or magnesium, which can be remedied by applying an appropriate fertilizer.

The leaves are distorted

Roses are particularly sensitive to all forms of hormonal herbicide, such as glyphosate and selective weed killers applied to lawns. They shouldn't be used at all in the garden, but if you absolutely must, keep them well away from your roses, and avoid applying them when the wind is blowing in

Powdery mildew

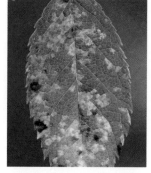

Rust

Mottling (caused by leaf hoppers)

Leaf hoppers

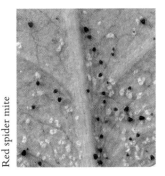

Red spider mite

Chlorosis

Hormonal weedkiller damage

Balling

their direction. The symptoms are easy to identify: the leaves become much smaller and the leaflets very narrow. Depending on the size of the dose, the rose may or may not survive.

The flowers won't open

This is known as "balling". It happens in wet weather, soft-petalled varieties with many petals being more susceptible to it. You may be able to save the flower by pulling off the confining outer petals, so releasing the inner ones. Once the weather has improved, new flowers will open normally.

The best remedies

We all want a magic answer when a favourite plant is attacked, but I would advocate patience and good gardening methods as better long-term solutions to any problems your roses have.

Natural solutions

Following the suggestions on p.223, and taking the best care you can of your soil and all the plants in your garden is the organic approach to solving these problems. A liquid foliar feed (seaweed, garlic, or similar), applied regularly even before any problems are visible, may be the best medicine for most diseases. It's difficult to produce perfectly pest- and disease-free roses; better to accept and live with low levels, and know that in the case of pests they're supplying food for the other wildlife in your garden.

Using chemicals

Chemical controls should be considered a last resort. In some countries fungicides and pesticides are available for controlling specific problems, but they need to be used with care as they can have harmful effects on the environment. Fungicides against diseases such as black spot and mildew should be used as a preventative, and pesticides only when the chances of harming any other insects is non-existent. Always use them on a still day, so you can control where they land, and take care to protect yourself and your pets from any contact with them.

Glossary

Annual
A plant that completes its life cycle, from germination to flowering, seeding, and then death, in one growing season.

Bare-root
A nursery-grown plant sold with no soil or container. Usually sold in winter, when the plant is dormant.

Budding
See grafting.

Containerized
A nursery-grown plant sold in a container with compost.

Cross-pollination
When pollen from one plant fertilizes the flower of another, producing a hybrid variety.

Cutting
A section of a plant that is removed and used for propagation (p.212).

Dead-head
To remove spent flower heads in order to promote further growth or flowering, or to improve the plant's appearance.

Double flower
A form of flower with at least 30 petals, and with the stamens absent or not visible (at least initially).

Fully double flower
A form of flower with at least 60 petals, often giving a rosette appearance, and with the stamens absent or or obscured, even when the bloom is fully open.

Grafting
A technique used by commercial growers, by which an artificial union is made between two plants. The bud of the desired plant is grafted on to the rootstock of another, in order to encourage strong growth and produce a large plant quickly (p.212).

Hardiness
How resistant a plant is to cold. Hardiness rating systems differ between countries; for example, in the UK, the RHS use "H" numbers, while in the US, USDA zones are used.

Hardy
Plants that are able to withstand outdoor conditions year-round, including temperatures below freezing, without protection.

Hips
The fruit of a rose plant, which contains the rose's seed. Typically produced in autumn, the brightly coloured hips can provide both late-season interest and a source of food for birds.

Layering
A method of propagation in which a stem is induced to root by being pegged down into the soil, while still attached to the parent plant (p.212).

Mulch
A layer of organic material, such as manure, compost, or wood chips, applied to the top of soil in order to help retain moisture, suppress weeds, and protect and feed the soil.

NPK
Short for "nitrogen, phosphorus, potassium", the nutritional breakdown of fertilizer, typically expressed as a ratio (e.g. 5:5:10).

Perennial
A plant that lives for at least three seasons. Also known as "herbaceous perennials", they die down at the end of each growing season.

pH
The level of acidity or alkalinity of soil or compost depicted on a scale from 1 to 14, which can be assessed using a testing kit (p.208). Roses need soil to be close to neutral (pH7), typically in the 6–7.5 range.

Rejuvenate
To cut all stems back hard to near ground level, in order to encourage new shoots to grow from the base. Normally done to a rose that has not been pruned properly for a number of years.

Root ball
The roots and accompanying soil or compost visible when a plant is lifted.

Rootstock
A plant used to provide the root system for a grafted (budded) plant.

Semi-double flower
A form of flower with more petals than a single flower (usually 8–14).

Single flower
A form of flower with one row of usually 5–7 petals, or as few as 4 petals in exceptional cases.

Species rose
A naturally occuring type; also known as a wild rose (p.64).

Specimen
A plant with a striking shape that looks good on its own or as a centerpiece of a larger display.

Standard
A shrub grafted on to a rootstock with a clear length of stem below the graft, lifting the rose up to make a tree-like shape.

Sucker
A shoot that arises from below ground level, directly from the roots. Grafted (budded) roses may occasionally produce suckers from the rootstock, which need to be removed (p.225).

Training
A method of guiding the direction of a plant's growth by arranging and securing its stems, in order to encourage more flowers and better coverage of a surface.

Tender
A plant that is sensitive to frost.

Resources

Organizations and online resources

For more information about specific rose varieties, find a local rose society, or to become involved with rose conservation, take a look at these organisations and resources.

Royal Horticultural Society
www.rhs.org.uk

Combined Rose List:
The International Rose Directory (updated annually)
www.combinedroselist.com

Historic Roses Group
historicroses.org

Help Me Find
helpmefind.com/rose/plants

Plant Heritage
plantheritage.org.uk

The Rose Society UK
therosesociety.org.uk

Roses UK
rosesuk.com

World Federation of Rose Societies
www.worldrose.org

UK nurseries and suppliers

A reputable supplier is a must when sourcing roses for your garden. I recommend looking into the following nurseries as a starting point for your search.

David Austin Roses
davidaustinroses.co.uk

Apuldram Roses
apuldramroses.co.uk

Harkness Roses
roses.co.uk

Peter Beales
classicroses.co.uk/roses

Pocock's Roses
garden-roses.co.uk

Style Roses
styleroses.co.uk

Trevor White Roses
trevorwhiteroses.co.uk

European nurseries and suppliers

While UK nurseries can supply a great deal of varieties, some roses may need to be sourced from further afield. If your search of UK suppliers does not provide the specific variety you are seeking, check out one of the following recommended Continental nurseries to see if they have the one you're looking for.

Flora Linnea (Sweden)
floralinnea.se/rosor

Kordes Roses (Germany)
rosen.de/en

Lens Roses (Belgium)
lens-roses.com
Meilland (France)
meilland.com/en

Rosenpark Draeger (Germany)
www.rosenpark-draeger.de

Roseposten (Denmark)
www.rosenposten.dk

Roses Loubert (France)
pepiniere-rosesloubert.com

Recommended further reading

Book of Perennials, Claire Austin (White Hopton Publications, 2020)

The English Roses, David Austin (ACC Art Books, 2021)

The English Roses, David Austin (Conran Octopus 2017)

The Rose, David Austin (Garden Art Press, 2013)

Pests, Diseases & Disorders of Garden Plants, Stefan Buczacki and Keith Harris (Collins, 2014)

Tea Roses, Lynn Chapman et al (Rosenberg Publishing, 2008)

Rosor för nordiska trädgårdar, Lars-Åke Gustavsson (Natur och Kultur 1999)

Compendium of Rose Diseases, R. Kenneth Horst (American Phytopathological Society, 2007)

Rosa: The Story of the Rose, Peter Kukielski with Charles Philips (Yale University Press, 2021)

Roses Without Chemicals, Peter Kukielski (Timber Press, 2015)

The Gardener's Book of Colour, Andrew Lawson (Pimpernel Press, 2015)

Scots Roses, Mary McMurtrie (Garden Art Press, 1999)

By Any Other Name: A Cultural History of the Rose, Simon Morley (Oneworld, 2021)

The Ultimate Guide to Roses, Roger Phillips and Martyn Rix (Macmillan, 2004)

The Rose, Jennifer Potter (Atlantic Books, 2011)

RHS Encyclopaedia of Roses, Charles Quest-Ritson and Brigid Quest-Ritson (DK, 2008)

The Rose Doctor, Gary Ritchie (2019)

Encyclopedia of Rose Science, ed. Dr Andrew Roberts

The English Flower Garden, William Robinson (Bloomsbury, 1998)

The History of the Rose in Denmark, Torben Thim (Centifolia, 2018)

The Graham Stuart Thomas Rose Book (John Murray, 1994)

Everyday Roses, Paul Zimmerman (Taunton Press, 2013)

Roses in Bermuda, Bermuda Rose Society Book Committee (2013)

Index

Page numbers in *italics*
refer to illustrations

A
animals 226–27
aphids 59, 226, *226*
arches 40
   roses for 182–91
Asia, roses in 8–10
Austin, David 13, 14, 82
autumn, roses for 46–47

B
balling 229, *229*
bare-root roses 206, *207*, 209, 211
Bennett, Henry 62–63
black spot 227, *227*
borders
   roses for the back of borders
     102–107
   roses for the front of borders
     90–95
   roses for the middle of borders
     96–101
   roses for mixed borders 108–17
Bourbon roses 73, *73*

C
care of roses 204–29
Cercospora fungi 227–28, *227*
Champney, John 84
China 8, 14
China roses 8, 72, *72*
chlorosis 228, *229*
climbing roses 36, 42, 47, 84–85
   companions for 43–45
   growing in containers 211
   pruning 220
   training 222, *222*
colour effects 30–33
containers 48–49
   roses for 118–23
cut flowers 152–57
cuttings 212, *213*

D
damask roses 69, 71
dead-heading 216, *216*
diseases and pests 18, 223, 226–29

downy mildew 227, *227*
drainage 224

E
English roses 19, 49, 52, 82, *82*
Europe, roses in 11

F
feeding 215
fences 36–41
   roses for 192–97
   training against 222, *222*
floribunda roses 18, 19, 24, 77, 77
   in containers 49
   mixed planting 29
   pruning 218
fruity fragrances 14
fungicides 18, 229

G
ground cover roses 83, *83*
growth, poor 224–25
Guillot, Jean-Baptiste 75

H
hedges 34–35, 53
   roses for 164–69
height, adding 23
herbicides 228, *229*
hips 23, 47, 57–59, 64
   roses for 158–63
hybrid musks 80, *80*
hybrid perpetuals 74, *74*, 76
hybrid species roses 64–71, 218
hybrid tea roses 18, 19, 24, 63, 76, *76*
   mixed planting 29
   pruning 218

K
Kordes 81

L
Lacharme, François 62
layering 212
leaf-cutter bee 226, *227*
leaf hoppers 228, *228*

leaf-rolling sawfly 226, *226*
leaves
   pests and diseases 226–29
   roses for 158–63
   scent 14
Lens, Louis 80

M

meadows with roses 53–57
miniature roses 24, 49, 79, *79*
mixed borders 18, 24–31
   colour effects 30–33
   combining plants 27–29
   planning 24–27
   roses for 108–17
modern roses 76–83
Moore, Ralph 79
mosses 14, 71
mulching 214
musk fragrance 14
myrrh fragrance 13

N

nature, inspired by 52–59
neglected roses, rejuvenating 221
Noisette, Philippe 84
noisettes 84, *84*

O

obelisks 22, 41–42
   roses for 182–91
old roses, fragrance 12–13

P

patio roses 24, 49, 78, *79*
Paul, William 62
Pemberton, Reverend Joseph
   80
pergolas 23, 41
   roses for 182–91
Perichon, Monsieur 73
pesticides 18, 229
pests and diseases 18, 59, 223,
   226–29
pillars 22, 41–42
   roses for 182–91
planting roses 23, 209–11

transplanting 211
   where to plant 207–208
plants
   combining 27–29
   mixed borders 24–31
polyantha roses 49, 75, *75*
Portland roses 19, 74, *74*
Poulsen, D. T. 77
powdery mildew 228, *228*
propagating roses 212–13
pruning 217–22, 223
   how to prune 217–20
   when to prune 220–21

R

Radler, Bill 81
rambling roses 42–43, 47, 51,
   58, 85, *85*
   pruning and training 220
red spider mites 228, *229*
rejuvenating roses 221
remedies 229
repeat-flowering roses 72–75
   pruning 218–20, *219*
Repton, Humphry 18
Robinson, William 24
Rosa
   R. 'Absolutely Fabulous' 125, *125*
   R. 'Adélaïde d'Orléans' 42, 53,
     85, 200, *201*
   R. 'Aglaia' *188*, 189
   R. 'Alaska' 187, *187*
   R. × *alba* 70
   R. × *alba* 'Alba Semiplena' 48,
     52, 56, 70, *70*
   R. 'The Albrighton Rambler'
     190, *191*
   R. 'Allegro' 186, *186*
   R. 'Amadeus' 194, *194–95*
   R. 'American Pillar' 200, *201*
   R. 'The Ancient Mariner' 42,
     150, *151*
   R. *arvensis* 13, 85
   R. 'Athena' 155, *155*
   R. 'Ballerina' *22*, 33, 52
   R. *bankside* 'Lutea' 202, *202*
   R. 'Bathsheba' 195, *195*

R. 'Bee's Paradise White' 134, *134*
R. 'Belle de Jour' 112, *112*
R. 'Blush Noisette' 84, *84*
R. 'Blush Rambler' 202, *202–203*
R. 'Bonica' *47*, 48, 51, 58
R. 'Boscobel' *142*, 143
R. *bracteata* 64, *64*
R. 'Buttercup' 33, 143, *143*
R. 'Buxom Beauty' 155, *155*
R. *californica* 48, 56
R. *c.* 'Plena' 103, *103*
R. *canina* 56, 57, 64, 70, 136, *137*
R. 'Caroline's Heart' 29, 80, 99, *99*
R. 'Cécile Brünner' 75, *75*
R. 'Céline Forestier' 145, *145*
R. 'Celsiana' 51, 52, 69, *69*
R. × *centifolia* 70
R. × *centifolia* 'Fantin-Latour' 70, *70*
R. × *centifolia* 'Muscosa' 71
R. 'Centre Stage' 52, 83
R. 'Champagne Moment' 23,
   100, *101*
R. 'Chandos Beauty' 154, *154*
R. 'Chawton Cottage' 179, *179*
R. 'Chevy Chase' 178, *179*
R. *chinensis* 8, 14
R. 'Cinderella' 104, *104–105*
R. 'City of York' 178, *178*
R. 'Clair Matin' 33, 52, 107, *107*
R. 'Claire Austin' *192*, 193
R. 'Climbing Cécile Brunner' 42,
   200, *201*
R. 'Climbing Étoile de Hollande'
   171, *171*
R. 'Climbing Lady Hillingdon' 75,
   75, 174, *174*
R. 'Climbing Madame Caroline
   Testout' *85*, 180, 181
R. 'Climbing Mrs Herbert Stevens'
   175, *175*
R. 'Complicata' 56, 138, *139*
R. 'Comte de Chambord' 74, 97, *97*
R. 'Comte de Champagne' 52,
   130, 131
R. 'Constance Spry' 13, 82, 146, *146*
R. 'Cornelia' 80, *102*, 103
R. 'Crème Chantilly' 166, *166*

R. 'Crimson Siluetta' 189, *189*

R. 'Crown Princess Margareta' 186, *186*

R. 'Desdemona' 18, 48, 82, *108*, 109, *122*, 123

R. 'Dolomiti' 125, *125*

R. 'Empereur Charles IV' 18, 30, *92*, 93

R. 'Eustacia Vye' 29, 30, 82, *108*, 109, 142, *142*

R. *fedtschenkoana* 58, 64, 69

R. 'Felicia' *51*, 80, *110*, 111

R. 'Ferdinand Pichard' 74, *74*

R. *filipes* 'Kiftsgate' 58, 85, 199, *199*

R. 'For Your Eyes Only' 116, *117*

R. 'Fortuna' *134–35*, 135

R. 'Francis E. Lester' 42, 53, 58, 85,199, *199*

R. 'Fruity Parfuma' 29, 48

R. 'Gabriel Oak' 82, 100, *101*

R. *gallica* 12, 49, 56, 68, 69, 70

R. *g.* 'Charles de Mills' 68, *68*

R. *g.* 'Ipsilanté' 68, 113, *113*

R. *g.* 'Président de Sèze' *62*, 68

R. *g.* 'Tuscany Superb' 68, 112, *112*

R. *g.* var. *officinalis* 52, 62, 68, 74, 116, *117*

R. *g.* 'Versicolor' 52, 68

R. 'Gartenprinzessin Marie-José' 121, *121*

R. 'The Generous Gardener' 58, 162, *162*, 171, *171*

R. 'Geranium' 56, 162, *163*

R. 'Gertrude Jekyll' *32–33*, 36, 45, *51*, 82, *82*, 88, *89*, 146, *147*, 172, *172*

R. 'Ghislaine de Féligonde' 36, 172, *172–73*

R. *glauca* 59, 64, *64*, 153, *153*

R. 'Golden Beauty' 18, 29, *122*, 123

R. 'Golden Gate' 36, 174, *174–75*

R. 'Goldspatz' 35, 166, *166*

R. 'Graham Thomas' 82, 144, *144*, 193, *193*

R. 'Great Maiden's Blush' 115, *115*

R. 'Guirlande d'Amour' 80, *196–97*, 197

R. 'Harlow Carr' 109, *109*, 168, *168*

R. 'Hella' 176, *176*

R. 'Herzogin Christiana' 120, *120*

R. *hugonis* 49, 136, *136*

R. 'Hyde Hall' 104, *104*

R. 'Iceberg' 29, 77, 77

R. 'Île de Fleurs' 34, 35, 52, 81, 166, *166*

R. 'Ispahan' 24, 51, 69, 146, *146*

R. 'Jacques Cartier' 74, 144, *144*

R. 'James Galway' 180, *181*

R. 'James L. Austin' 28, *156–57*, 157

R. 'Jasmina' 186, *186*

R. 'Joie de Vivre' 51, 121, *121*

R. 'Katharina Zeimet' *128–29*, 129

R. 'Kew Gardens' 51, 167, *167*

R. 'Kew Rambler' *198*, 199

R. 'Königin von Dänemark' 149, *149*

R. 'La Ville de Bruxelles' 100, *101*

R. 'Lady Emma Hamilton' *148–49*, 149

R. 'The Lady Gardener' 28, 34, 42, 111, *111*, 118, *118*

R. 'The Lady of the Lake' 42, 53, 85, *170*, 171

R. 'Lady of Shalott' 24, *35*, 36, 57–58, 97, *97*, 195, *195*

R. 'The Lady's Blush' 52, 57, 135, *135*

R. 'Laguna' 190, *191*

R. 'Lampion' *158*, 159

R. 'The Lark Ascending' 33, 103, *103*, 164, *164*

R. 'Lavender Siluetta' 175, *175*, 188, *188*

R. 'Leverkusen' 178, *178*

R. 'Lichfield Angel' 111, *111*

R. 'Louise Odier' 73, *73*

R. 'Lovely Parfuma' 18, 29, 94, *95*

R. 'Lupo' 52, 126, *127*

R. 'Lynda Bellingham' 154, *154–55*

R. 'Madame Alfred Carrière' 84, 176, *177*

R. 'Madame Hardy' 69, 110, *110*

R. 'Madame Legras de Saint Germain' 150, *151*

R. 'Madame Plantier' 62, 175, *175*

R. 'Maid of Kent' 187, *187*

R. 'Malvern Hills' 183, *183*

R. 'Marie Pavié' 75, 123, *123*

R. 'Mary Wallace' *38–39*

R. 'Milhem Pemberton' 93, *93*

R. 'Miss Edith Cavell' 75, 126, *127*

R. 'Molineux' 93, *93*

R. 'Morning Mist' 33, 52, 132, *133*

R. 'Mortimer Sackler' 89, *192*, 193

R. *moschata* 69, 84

R. *moyesii* 47, 56, 64

R. *mundi* 52, 68

R. 'Munstead Wood' *51*, 145, *145*

R. 'Narrow Water' *182*, 183

R. 'Natasha Richardson' 29, 120, *120–21*

R. *nitida* 46, 56

R. 'Nuits de Young' 71, 113, *113*

R. *nutkana* 56, 62, 138, *139*

R. × *odorata* 'Mutabilis' 30, 33, 45, 46, 72, *72*

R. 'Olivia Rose Austin' 18, 29, 51, 116, *117*, 168, *168–69*

R. 'Open Arms' 42, 49, 53, 194, *194*

R. *palustris* 48, 56, 62, 140, *140*

R. 'Paul Noël' 43, 184, *184–85*

R. 'Paula Vapelle' 98, *98*

R. 'Paul's Himalayan Musk' 143, *143*

R. 'Pearl Drift' 94, *95*

R. 'Penelope' 33, 52, 80, *80*, *106–107*, 107

R. 'The Pilgrim' 180, *181*

R. 'Pink Hit' *128*, 129

R. 'Pink Roadrunner' 52, 167, *167*

R. 'Polyantha Grandiflora' 53, 58, 132, *133*

R. 'Portlandica' 74, *74*

R. 'Pour Toi' 79, *79*

R. 'Pride of England' 155, *155*

R. *primula* 56, 141, *141*

R. 'Princess Alexandra of Kent' 23, *96*, 97, 118, *119*

R. 'Princess Anne' 114, *114–15*

R. 'Prins Alexander' 94, *95*

R. 'Purple Skyliner' 36, 180, *181*, 185, *185*

R. 'Quatre Saisons' 69, 73, 74, 150, *151*

R. 'Queen of Sweden' 18, 28, 34, *152*, 153, 164, *165*

R. 'Rambling Rector' *41*, 53, 85, *85*, 150, *151*, 200, *201*

R. 'Rambling Rosie' 40, 42, 49, 190, *191*

R. × *richardii* 48, 132, *133*

R. 'Roald Dahl' 82, 90, *91*, 153, *153*

R. 'Rose de Rescht' 74, 144, *144*

R. 'Rosy Cushion' 81, *81*

R. *rubiginosa* 14, 56, 59, *59*, 160, *160*

R. *rugosa* 34, 46, 47, 48, 56, 58, 64, 66, 207

R. *r.* 'Alba' 161, *161*

R. *r.* 'Hansa' 66, 147, *147*

R. *r.* 'Roseraie de l'Hay' 66, *66*

R. 'Scarborough Fair' 52, 92, *92*

R. 'Scarlet Fire' 161, *161*

R. 'Scent from Heaven' 40, 183, *183*

R. 'Scented Carpet' 52, 83

R. *sericea* 47, 56, 58, 64

R. *s.* subsp. *omeiensis* f. *pteracantha* 159, *159*

R. 'The Shepherdess' 113, *113*

R. 'Sibelius' 29, 30, 80, 121, *121*

R. 'Silas Marner' 157, *157*

R. 'Sophie's Perpetual' 145, *145*

R. 'Sourire d'Isabelle' 197, *197*

R. *spinosissima* 23, 45, 48, 56, 64, 67, *162*, 162, 207

R. *s.* 'Dunwich Rose' 67, 131, *131*

R. *s.* 'Grandiflora' 46

R. *s.* 'Single Cherry' 67, 138, *139*

R. *s.* 'William III' 67, *67*

R. 'Stéphanie d'Ursel' 30, 112, *112*

R. 'Sternenhimmel' *128*, 129

R. 'Summer of Love' 126, *127*

R. 'Summer Memories' 30, 42, 81, 114, *114*

R. 'Summertime' 190, *191*

R. 'Sunny Siluetta' 189, *189*

R. 'Super Fairy' 184, *184*

R. 'Sweet Haze' 94, *95*

R. 'Sweet Honey' *124*, 125

R. *sweginzowii* 47, 56, 141, *141*

R. 'Thérèse Bugnet' 105, *105*

R. 'Thomas à Becket' 98, *98–99*, 167, *167*

R. 'Topolina' 56–57, 132, *133*

R. 'Tottering-by-Gently' 33, *53*, 56–57, 116, *117*, *158*, 159

R. 'Treasure Trove' 203, *203*

R. 'Trier' 52, 80

R. 'Vanessa Bell' 100, *101*

R. 'Vanity' 33, 52

R. 'Violacea' 56, 105, *105*

R. *virginiana* 46, 56, 138, *139*

R. 'Warm Welcome' 187, *187*

R. 'Warm Wishes' 76, *76*

R. 'Weg der Sinne' *130*, 131

R. 'Westerland' 105, *105*

R. 'White Flower Carpet' 23, 83, *83*

R. 'A White Shade of Pale' 90, *90*

R. 'Wildfire' 126, *127*

R. 'William Lobb' 71, *71*, *160*, 161

R. 'Wollerton Old Hall' 195, *195*

R. *xanthina* 'Canary Bird' 56, *140*, 141

rose gardens 18–23

rose replant disease 224

rose sawfly 226, *226*

roses

buying 88, 206

care of 204–29

history of 8–11, 62–63

propagating 212–13

replacing 209

types of 60–85

where to plant 207–208

rust 228, *228*

S

scent 12–15

roses for 142–51

seeds, growing from 213

shade 50–51

semi-shady walls 176–81

shrub roses 24, 28, 211

modern 81, *81*

pruning 218–20, *219*

shrubberies 33

slug worms 226, *226*

soil 223, 224, 225

poor 48

preparing 208–209

species roses 58, 64–71, 218

stems

marks on 227

unusual stems 225

sun 224

warm, sunny walls 170–75

supporting roses 36

T

tea fragrance 14

tea roses 75, *75*, 76, 218

temperatures, extreme 49

thorns, roses for 158–63

tight spaces, roses for 124–29

training roses 217–22

transplanting 211

trees, growing through 42–45

roses for 198–203

V

Velle, Rudy and Ann 80

W

walls 23, 36–41

roses for 170–81, 192–97

training roses against 222, *222*

watering 215

weeding 214

wild areas, roses for 136–41

wild gardens 52–53

wild roses 52

wildlife, roses for 57–59, 130–35

winter 49

roses for 46–47

Acknowledgments

Author acknowledgments

My thanks to Chris Young for suggesting that I should write this book and then to my partner Rosie Irving who, despite my hesitation, persuaded me that it would be a good idea and then for her continued positivity.

Also to the DK team for bringing the book together so beautifully. They include Ruth O'Rourke, Amy Slack, Jane Birdsell, Emily Hedges, Vicky Read, and Glenda Fisher.

For getting me into the world of roses, I owe a huge amount of thanks to the late David Austin who, despite my very limited knowledge at the time, took me on as nursery manager.

In the rose world there are many to thank with whom I have discussed roses in all their great diversity. They include Richard Stubbs and Stephen Parnham of David Austin Roses, Thomas Proll of Kordes Roses, John Anthony chairman of the Rose Society UK, Charles and Brigid Quest-Ritson, and Paul Zimmerman of Paul Zimmerman Roses.

Publisher acknowledgments

For their help in sourcing and providing images for the book, DK would like to thank Howard Rice, Eriko Nakakawaji, Thomas Proll (Kordes Roses), and Stephen Parnham. Thanks also to Francesco Piscitelli for proofreading, Vanessa Bird for indexing, and Vagisha Pushp for preparing picture credits.

Picture credits

The publisher would like to thank the following for their kind permission to reproduce their photographs:

(Key: **a**-above; **b**-below/bottom; **c**-centre; **f**-far; **l**-left; **r**-right; **t**-top)

2-3 Clive Nichols: Wynyard Hall, County Durham. **9 Bridgeman Images. 10 Bridgeman Images**: © Fitzwilliam Museum). **13 Alamy Stock Photo**: Artepics. **15 Bridgeman Images**: by courtesy of Julian Hartnoll. **19 Howard Rice**: The David Austin Rose Gardens, Shropshire, UK. **20-21 Clive Nichols**: Glyndebourne, East Sussex. The Mary Christie Rose Garden. **22 Howard Rice**: Hatton Grange, Shropshire, UK. **25 Clive Nichols**: André Eve Garden, France. **26 Yokohama English Garden**: Y. Sakurano. **28 Clive Nichols**: Manor Farm, Cheshire. **30 Marianne Majerus. 31 Howard Rice. 32 Clive Nichols. 34 © Andrea Jones/Garden Exposures Photo Library. 35 Jonathan Buckley. 37 © Andrea Jones/Garden Exposures Photo Library. 38-39 Hervé Lenain**: Les Jardins de Roquelin. **40 Alamy Stock Photo**: Michael Wheatley Photography. **41 Marianne Majerus**: Design: Rupert Wheeler and Paul Gazerwitz. **43 Yokohama English Garden**: Y. Sakurano. **44 Carolyn Parker. 46 © Andrea Jones/Garden Exposures Photo Library. 47 Clive Nichols**: Ellicar Gardens, near Doncaster. **50 © Andrea Jones/ Garden Exposures Photo Library. 51 Rachel Warne**: Design Jo Thompson. **53 Howard Rice. 54-55 Clive Nichols**: Rockcliffe Garden, Gloucestershire. **57 Alamy Stock Photo**: Lioneska. **58 © Andrea Jones/Garden Exposures Photo Library. 59 GAP Photos. 62 bl GAP Photos**: Howard Rice / Cambridge University Botanic Gardens; **bc GAP Photos**: Jonathan Buckley; **br GAP Photos**: Nova Photo Graphik. **63 Clive Nichols**: Mottisfont Abbey, Hampshire. **64 bl GAP Photos**: Michael Howes. **64 cl GAP Photos**: Ian Thwaites. **65 Howard Rice. 66 GAP Photos**: Carole Drake / Garden: Westbrook House, Somerset; Owners and Designers: Keith Anderson and David Mendel. **67 GAP Photos**: Nicola Stocken. **68 GAP Photos**: Christa Brand. **69 GAP Photos**: Keith Burdett. **70 cl GAP Photos**: Howard Rice, **b** Jonathan Buckley. **71 Jonathan Buckley. 72 GAP Photos. 73 Marianne Majerus**: Design Rachel Bebb. **74 tl GAP Photos**: Christina Bollen; **cl GAP Photos**: Howard Rice. **75 cr GAP Photos**: Howard Rice; **br GAP Photos**: Richard Bloom. **76 David Austin Roses. 77 Marianne Majerus**: Design: Acres Wild. **78 Marianne Majerus. 79 GAP Photos**: Howard Rice. **80 Marianne Majerus**: Rymans, Sussex. **81 GAP Photos**: Howard Rice / Location: The Manor House, Stevington. **82 John Glover. 83 Marianne Majerus**: Design: Dominick Murphy, Ireland. **84 cl GAP Photos**: Howard Rice; **bl © Andrea Jones/Garden Exposures Photo Library. 85 © Andrea Jones/Garden Exposures Photo Library. 89 Rachel Warne**: Design: Jo Thompson. **90 GAP Photos**: Fiona Lea. **91 GAP Photos**: Howard Rice. **92 t Lens Roses; b Alamy Stock Photo**: Lindsay Constable. **93 cr David Austin Roses; br Lens Roses. 95 tl GAP Photos**: Ron Evans; **tr GAP Photos**: Richard Wareham; **bl Lens Roses; br Kordes Roses. 96 Howard Rice**: Wynyard Hall Rose Garden, County Durham, UK. **97 cra GAP Photos**: Howard Rice; **br Alamy Stock Photo**: Avalon.red. **98 bl Lens Roses. 98-99 Marianne Majerus**: Parc Thermal de Mondorf-les-Bains, Luxembourg. **99 br Lens Roses. 101 tr GAP Photos**: Howard Rice / David Austin Roses; **tr Clive Nichols**: André Eve Rose Nursery, France; **bl GAP Photos**: J S Sira; **br David Austin Roses. 102 Marianne Majerus. 103 t GAP Photos**: Carole Drake - Garden: Westbrook House, Somerset; Owners and Designers: Keith Anderson and David Mendel; **b GAP Photos**: Howard Rice. **104 tl GAP Photos**: Howard Rice; **tr Kordes Roses. 105 l Marianne Majerus; c Getty Images / iStock / schnuddel r GAP Photos**: Tim Gainey. **106-107 Marianne**

Majerus: Design: Acres Wild. **107 br David Austin Roses. 108 tl GAP Photos**: Joanna Kossak / Designer: Claudia de Yong; **br GAP Photos**: Dave Zubraski. **109 GAP Photos**: Howard Rice / Wynyard Hall Rose Garden, Stockton-on-Tees. **110 t GAP Photos**: Richard Bloom; **bl Botanikfoto**: Steffen Hauser. **111 t GAP Photos**: Rob Whitworth **111 b GAP Photos**: Jonathan Buckley. **112 tl Marianne Majerus**: Helmingham Hall, Suffolk; **tc Lens Roses**; **tr BARB**: Pépinières Georges Delbard. **113 tl GAP Photos**: Jo Whitworth; **tc David Austin Roses**; **tr Howard Rice. 114 bl GAP Photos**: Richard Wareham. **114–115 Clive Nichols**: Wynyard Hall, County Durham. **115 br Alamy Stock Photo**: Matthew Taylor. **117 tl GAP Photos; tr and bl © Andrea Jones/Garden Exposures Photo Library; br GAP Photos**: Sonia Hunt. **118 GAP Photos**: Jonathan Buckley. **119 GAP Photos**: Howard Rice. **120 tl Kordes Roses; tr GAP Photos**: Visions. **121 tl Marianne Majerus; tc © Andrea Jones/Garden Exposures Photo Library; tr Kordes Roses. 122 t Kordes Roses; b David Austin Roses. 123 GAP Photos**: Howard Rice. **124 Kordes Roses. 125 t Harkness Roses; b GAP Photos**: Richard Wareham. **127 tl GAP Photos**: Friedrich Strauss; **tr GAP Photos**:Tim Gainey; **bl Kordes Roses; br GAP Photos. 128 cl Kordes Roses; bl GAP Photos**: FhF Greenmedia. **128–129 GAP Photos**: Clive Nichols / André Eve Rose Nursery, France. **130 t GAP Photos**: Howard Rice; **b Kordes Roses. 131 GAP Photos**: Tommy Tonsberg. **133 tl GAP Photos**: Julie Dansereau; **t Howard Rice; bl GAP Photos**: Jacqui Dracup; **br Kordes Roses. 134 bl Rosen Tantau; 134–135 GAP Photos**: Robert Mabic. **135 br GAP Photos**: Jonathan Need. **136 Botanikfoto**: Hans-Roland Mülle. **137 Shutterstock. com**: mcajan. **139 tl GAP Photos**: Pernilla Bergdahl; **tr and bl GAP Photos**: Howard Rice; **br Alamy Stock Photo**: Sharon Talson. **140 t GAP Photos**: Howard Rice / Madingley Hall, Cambridge; **b Marianne Majerus. 141 t Shutterstock.com**: Jiang Tianmu; **b GAP Photos**: Zara Napier. **142 t GAP Photos**: Nicola Stocken; **br Jonathan Buckley. 143 t GAP Photos**: Jonathan Buckley; **b Howard Rice. 144 tl GAP Photos**: Rob Whitworth; **tc GAP photos**: Ellen Rooney; **tr GAP Photos John Glover. 145 tl GAP Photos**: Nicola Stocken; **tc David Austin Roses; tr GAP Photos**: Mark Bolton. **146 t GAP Photos**: Rob Whitworth; **b Marianne Majerus**: Bramdean House, Hampshire. **147 t GAP Photos**: Martin Hughes-Jones; **b GAP Photos**: Annie Green-Armytage. **148–149 Marianne Majerus**: Design: Acres Wild. **149 br GAP Photos**: Sabina Ruber. **151 tl Alamy Stock Photo**: Imagebroker; **tr Alamy Stock Photo**: Jane Tregelles; **bl GAP Photos**: Howard Rice; **br Shutterstock.com**: Sergey V Kalyakin. **152 GAP Photos**: Howard Rice. **153 tr Alamy Stock Photo**: flowerphotos; **b Sergey Kalyakin. 154 t Harkness Roses; b GAP Photos**:Jacqui Dracup. **155 tl Dreamstime.com**: André Muller; **tc Kordes Roses; tr GAP Photos**: Rachel Warne. **156–157 GAP Photos**: Jonathan Buckley / David Austin Roses. **157 br David Austin Roses. 158 t Lens Roses; b Stephen Parnham. 159 GAP Photos**: Howard Rice. **160 t Marianne Majerus; b Botanikfoto**: Hans-Roland Mülle. **161 t Marianne Majerus; b GAP Photos**: Martin Hughes-Jones. **162 t Michael Marriott; b GAP Photos**: Jonathan Buckley. **163 © Andrea Jones/Garden Exposures Photo Library**. **164 GAP Photos**: Howard Rice. **165 GAP Photos**: Howard Rice / Wynyard Hall Rose Garden, Stockton-on-Tees. **166 tl ©MEILLAND INTERNATIONAL; tc and tr Kordes Roses. 167 tl Alamy Stock Photo**: P Tomlins; **tc Jason Ingram; tr Kordes Roses. 168 bl Shutterstock.com**: Clickmanis. **168–169 Howard Rice. 170 GAP Photos**: Howard Rice. **171 t GAP Photos**: Maddie Thornhill; **b GAP Photos**: Nicola Stocken. **172 and 173 Marianne Majerus. 174 tl GAP Photos**: Howard Rice; **tr Alamy Stock Photo**: Jane Tregelles. **175 tl Alamy Stock Photo**: Organica; **tc Alamy Stock Photo**: Matteo Omied; **tr Kordes Roses. 176 Kordes Roses. 177 David Austin Roses. 178 t GAP Photos**: Heather Edwards; **b David Austin Roses. 179 t GAP Photos**: Christa Brand; **b Shutterstock.com**: Sergey V Kalyakin. **181 tl GAP Photos**: Geoff du Feu; **tr GAP Photos**: Ron Evans; **bl GAP Photos**: Tim Gainey; **br GAP Photos**: Ron Evans. **182 GAP Photos**: Carole Drake / Garden: Westbrook House, Somerset; Owners and Designers: Keith Anderson and David Mendel. **183 t GAP Photos**: Richard Wareham; **b GAP Photos**: Martin Hughes-Jones. **184 bl Alamy Stock Photo**: Deborah Vernon. **184–185 Jonathan Buckley. 185 br Shutterstock.com**: InfoFlowersPlants. **186 tl ©MEILLAND INTERNATIONAL; tc Kordes Roses; tr GAP Photos**: Howard Rice. **187 tl GAP Photos**: Tommy Tonsberg; **tc Kordes Roses; tr GAP Photos**: Nicola Stocken **188 t GAP Photos**: Lynn Keddie; **br Kordes Roses. 189 tr and br Kordes Roses. 191 tl Michael Marriott; tr GAP Photos**: Howard Rice / David Austin Rose Gardens, Albrighton, Wolverhampton; **bl Kordes Roses; br Howard Rice. 192 tl and bc GAP Photos**: Howard Rice. **193 GAP Photos**: Jacqui Dracup. **194 tl Jason Ingram; tr GAP Photos**: Nova Photo Graphik. **195 tl and tc Shutterstock.com**: Sergey V Kalyakin; **tr GAP Photos**: Jenny Lilly. **196–197 Marianne Majerus. 197 br Lens Roses. 198 GAP Photos**: Howard Rice / David Austin Rose Gardens, Shropshire. **199 tr GAP Photos**: Jonathan Buckley / David Austin Roses; **br GAP Photos**: Howard Rice. **201 tl Alamy Stock Photo**: blickwinkel / Dautel; **tr GAP Photos**: Howard Rice; **bl Marianne Majerus**: Design: Diann Grafton; **br Alamy Stock Photo**: Imagebroker / Arco / J. Pfeiffer. **202 bl GAP Photos**: Howard Rice. **202–203 GAP Photos**: Jonathan Buckley / David Austin Roses. **203 br GAP Photos**: Rob Whitworth. **226 t Nature Picture Library**: Nigel Cattlin; **ac Professor Stefan Buczacki; bc Howard Rice; b Minden Pictures**: Nigel Cattlin. **227 t Nature Picture Library**: Nick Upton; **ac Professor Stefan Buczacki; bc and b Kordes Roses. 228 t Professor Stefan Buczacki; ac GAP Photos**: Geoff Kidd; **bc Getty Images / iStock**: Natalya Vilman; **b Kordes Roses. 229 t Nature Picture Library**: Nigel Cattlin. **ac and b Howard Rice; bc Kordes Roses.**

Cover images: Front: **GAP Photos**: Joanna Kossak / Designer: Claudia de Yong; Back: **Howard Rice**

All other images © Dorling Kindersley

DK LONDON
Project Editor Amy Slack
Senior Designer Glenda Fisher
Editor Jane Birdsell
Designer Vicky Read
Picture Researcher Emily Hedges
Illustrator Vicky Read
Production Editor David Almond
Production Controller Rebecca Parton
Jacket Designer Maxine Pedliham
Jacket Editor Jasmin Lennie
Editorial Manager Ruth O'Rourke
Design Manager Marianne Markham
Consultant Gardening Publisher Chris Young
Art Director Maxine Pedliham
Publisher Katie Cowan

ROYAL HORTICULTURAL SOCIETY
Consultant Simon Maughan
Publisher Rae Spencer-Jones

First published in Great Britain in 2022 by
Dorling Kindersley Limited
DK, One Embassy Gardens, 8 Viaduct Gardens,
London, SW11 7BW

The authorised representative in the EEA is
Dorling Kindersley Verlag GmbH. Arnulfstr. 124,
80636 Munich, Germany

Copyright © 2022 Dorling Kindersley Limited
A Penguin Random House Company
Text copyright © 2022 Michael Marriott
10 9 8 7 6 5 4 3 2 1
001–327515–May/2022

A CIP catalogue record for this book
is available from the British Library.
ISBN: 978-0-2415-4389-4

Printed and bound in China

For the curious
www.dk.com

About the author

From a very young age, Michael Marriott has been a keen gardener, but it wasn't until he joined David Austin Roses in the mid-eighties that he became immersed in the world of roses. As an integral member of the nursery, he played an important role in the popularisation of the English Roses. He is passionate about roses in all their diversity, both as a central plant for the garden and as an important part of so many cultures around the world.

Michael has designed many thousands of rose gardens and borders around the world – private and public, large and small – including the Royal Botanic Gardens Kew, Queen Mary's Rose Garden in Regent's Park, Hampton Court Palace, Wynyard Hall, Trentham Gardens, the David Austin rose garden near Osaka, Japan and even a garden in Bhutan to celebrate the marriage of their King and Queen.

Michael frequently lectures, leads garden tours, and runs workshops both at home and abroad on all aspects of roses as well as writing for magazines. In 2020, he revised and updated David Austin's *The English Roses* (ACC Art Books).

At home, Michael and his partner, Rosie Irving, garden very much along organic lines, and this is something he is keen to pass onto anyone with roses in their garden.